# Jacques Cartier

ADAM WOOG

# GREAT EXPLORERS

Jacques Cartier

James Cook

Hernán Cortés

Sir Francis Drake

Vasco da Gama

Sir Edmund Hillary

Robert de La Salle

Lewis and Clark

Ferdinand Magellan

Sir Ernest Shackleton

# Jacques Cartier

ADAM WOOG

CHELSEA HOUSE PUBLISHERS
An imprint of Infobase Publishing

GREAT EXPLORERS: JACQUES CARTIER

Chelsea House
An imprint of Infobase Publishing
132 West 31st Street
New York, NY 10001

**Library of Congress Cataloging-in-Publication Data**
Woog, Adam, 1953-
  Jacques Cartier / Adam Woog.
    p. cm. — (Great explorers)
  Includes bibliographical references and index.
  ISBN 978-1-60413-430-8 (hardcover)
  1. Cartier, Jacques, 1491–1557—Juvenile literature. 2. Explorers—America—Biography—Juvenile literature. 3. Explorers—France—Biography—Juvenile literature. 4. Saint Lawrence River—Discovery and exploration—Jvenile literature, 5. Canada—Discovery and exploration—Juvenile lierature. 6. Canada—History—To 1763 (New France)—Juvenile literature. I. Title. II. Series.
  E133.C3W85 2009
  971.4'012—dc22            2009016267

Series design by Lina Farinella
Cover design by Keith Trego

Printed in the United States of America

Bang EJB 10 9 8 7 6 5 4 3 2 1

This book is printed on acid-free paper.

# CONTENTS

# Cartier and the Rush for Exploration

THE SIXTEENTH CENTURY WAS AN EXCITING TIME FOR EUROPE. One of the most thrilling activities during this age was the exploration of new territory. Many nations took part in a rush to discover riches, conquer foreign lands, and open new sea routes. In part, they made this dash hoping to take advantage of the unknown lands of North and South America.

One of the most important explorers of this era was Christopher Columbus. Columbus was not the first European to sail to the Western Hemisphere, but he was the first to achieve widespread fame for doing so. When his expedition stumbled on the Americas in 1492, his reports home launched a massive rush of exploration to the region.

Suddenly Europe became aware of a vast new world, one that was not part of the known European or Middle East civilizations and religions. Historian D.B. Quinn writes in *The Exploration of North America*, "In the sixteenth century, Europeans became aware rather suddenly that the world had opened up around them, that they were no longer confined to a relatively small Christian world and a somewhat hazy Muslim and pagan sphere around it."

## Early Exploration

When Columbus sailed across the Atlantic and discovered some of the islands of the Caribbean and the edges of South and Central America, he thought that he had reached India. Later explorers, such as Amerigo Vespucci, showed that this was not so. It seemed clear that the Americas were continents to themselves. It was also thought that Asia could not be reached by sailing west from Europe, as some people hoped.

In the next decades, many more European explorers crossed the Atlantic Ocean to the New World. Some were mainly interested in profiting from the gold and other valuables they hoped to find, especially in South America and the Caribbean. In this part of the hemisphere, voyagers sailing in the names of Spain, Holland, and Portugal controlled the bulk of the exploration, as well as the trade and domination of the native peoples there. Meanwhile, sailors and explorers from England and France concentrated mostly on the northeast coast of North America.

All of these voyages were paid for—as was virtually all exploration at the time—by the royal governments of certain countries. (The leaders of the expeditions often came from countries other than those that financed their trips. For example, Columbus was an Italian who sailed under the flag of Spain.)

In any case, it was a swift race and a ruthless business. In the foreword to *The Canadian Frontier*, historian Ray Allen Billington writes, "Almost from the day [when their early] outposts were established, each contending nation sought to extend its holdings into the territories of its rivals, using the three classic weapons in the arsenal of conquest: trade with the natives, diplomacy, and war."

## A Route to Asia

For the kings and queens who financed exploration of the New World, the process of acquiring riches and claiming new land for themselves was only part of their goal. Another major objective was to find a very specific sea route called the North-west Passage. This supposed route would lead through North

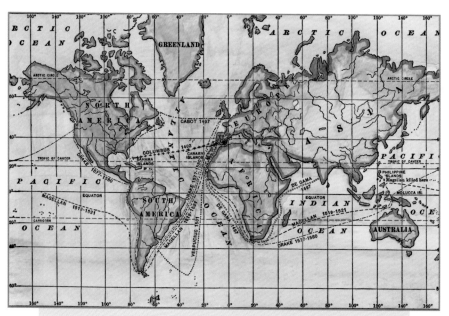

After Christopher Columbus's first expedition in 1492, European royals became fascinated with claiming parts of North America—the "New World"—for their own countries. Kings and queens, convinced there was a shorter route to the coveted spices and riches in Asia through the New World, funded transatlantic expeditions led by courageous sailors like Jacques Cartier. This began a period of unprecedented discovery as fearless explorers sailed throughout the world and discovered new lands, peoples, and cultures.

America all the way to the Pacific Ocean, providing a way to Asia.

It was important to find the Northwest Passage. A sea journey to Asia from Europe was long and treacherous and required sailing down the west coast of Africa, around its dangerous southern tip, and across the Indian Ocean. Still, even this long sea journey was preferable to a land journey through the Muslim nations of Southwest Asia, due to the poor relationship between them and the Christian nations of Europe.

Those sailors who did manage to navigate a round-trip by sea could make fortunes by bringing back treasures such as silk cloth and spices. Cinnamon, nutmeg, cloves, and other spices were so exotic and precious that they were often more valuable than gold to Europeans. A shorter, quicker, and safer path to Asia would thus give a nation an economic advantage over others.

## Exploration During the Renaissance

The Northwest Passage was not found, but the search for it was not a total failure. The explorers found many other things of wonder and value. Some of these were tangible treasures. The New World, at least South America, contained vast amounts of gold and other material riches. The booty brought back by the explorers further stimulated the European royalty's greed for wealth and conquest.

Exploration also expanded the imaginations of Europeans. This spirit of inquiry was a central part of the Renaissance, the great social and cultural movement of the time. The Renaissance was a wave of thought and action that brought Europe out of the Middle Ages (also called the medieval period or the Dark Ages) and allowed music, art, religion, and science to blossom as never before.

Developments in technology and science that came from the Renaissance were of immense help to the explorers of the New World. For example, there were dramatic advancements in astronomy (which aided in navigation) and improvements in telescopes, compasses, and firearms. Refinements in map-making and in shipbuilding, such as the development of large ocean-going ships with improved sails and other features, also helped tremendously.

## John Cabot

One of the explorers of the era who took advantage of these advances was an Italian named Giovanni Caboto, known as John Cabot by his royal British patrons. Cabot is generally acknowledged as the first European of the Renaissance era to discover and map North America. (A Norseman from Scandinavia, Leif Ericson, journeyed there much earlier—around the year 1003—but left no known maps.)

Cabot "discovered," among other things, the great island of Newfoundland, which is now part of Canada. It should be noted that the Europeans never "discovered" anything. The Amerindians or Indians, the native peoples who lived in the New World when the Europeans arrived, were, of course, already there. Nonetheless, the term "discovered" is commonly used. It indicates that the early European explorers were the first to map and describe the land in detail. In some cases, they were the first to create permanent settlements. Often, as is now acknowledged, this European exploration came at great expense to the aboriginal inhabitants.

Soon after Cabot reached Newfoundland, British, Spanish, and French fishermen began visiting the region regularly in search of its vast supply of codfish. One reason fish was in great demand was that France, Portugal, and Spain were overwhelmingly Catholic countries. The Church had mandated 153 "fish days" per year, days on which Catholics could eat only fish instead of meat, so there was a great demand for Newfoundland cod.

## Enter Jacques Cartier

Another important figure in the great race to explore North America and find the Northwest Passage was a Frenchman named Jacques Cartier. In some ways, Cartier was a failure. He did not succeed in finding the Northwest Passage, nor did he bring great riches such as diamonds or gold back to France. He also did not succeed in another of his goals: establishing a permanent settlement in Canada.

Yet, Cartier did accomplish a great deal. He was the first European to explore, describe, and map in detail the Gulf of St. Lawrence and a portion of the St. Lawrence River. This vast waterway proved to be a major passage into the interior of Canada, leading to the Great Lakes and other unexplored areas. Because of it, France was able to enter and build a vast colony in North America.

Cartier was also the first European to have a documented, proven meeting with the native North American tribes who lived along the river. He also was the first to record the use of the name *Canada*, which was originally a word in the language of the Iroquois, one of the tribes living in what is now the northeastern United States. The term *Canada* later came to refer to the vast nation of today. Because of these accomplishments, Cartier is considered one of the great heroes of Canadian and North American history.

## Born to Sail

Not much is known about Cartier's early life. A true-to-life portrait of him, one drawn during his life, does not even exist. The drawings and paintings that have survived may be rather fanciful. They show a stern, rather sad-looking, but still forceful man.

Jacques Cartier, one of the most celebrated French explorers in history, is best known for his expeditions to North America. Though he was famous in France, the details of his life remain a mystery, as official documents only list his parentage, marriage, and close relatives.

Historians do know that Cartier's parents were Jamet Cartier, a sea pilot, and his wife, Geseline Jansart. Jacques Cartier was born in Saint-Malo, France, in 1491, although the exact date is uncertain. Records indicate that he was baptized on the last day of December in 1491, so it is likely that he was born shortly before that date. Some records say Cartier was the second of five children, while others state that he was the youngest of three sons.

Saint-Malo, where he was born and raised, is a fortified seaport on the coast of Brittany, facing the English Channel. Brittany (called *Bretagne* in French) is a region in the northwest of what is now France. At the time of Cartier's birth, Brittany was a type of nation called a *duchy*, and was separate from France. It was incorporated into France in 1532.

Long before Cartier was born, Saint-Malo already had a strong reputation for its gifted navigators and sailors. Stephen Leacock, author of *The Mariner of Saint-Malo*, comments, "The situation of the port has made it a nursery for hardy seamen. . . . Here for centuries has dwelt a race of adventurous fishermen and navigators, whose daring is unsurpassed by any other seafaring people in the world." So it is not surprising—especially considering that his father was a sea pilot—that Cartier became a sailor.

Not much is known for sure about Cartier during his younger years. The only real evidence that remains from this period are a few mentions in civic documents listing him as a godfather to a child or as a witness in court cases. Still, historians can make some educated guesses about what his life was like. Cartier probably began going to sea at an early age, accompanying his father and the other sailors of Saint-Malo. It is also likely that he trained as a sailor and navigator at a famous naval school in Dieppe, another port on the northern coast of France.

## Cartier as a Young Man

In 1520, Cartier married Marie Catherine des Granches. The bride was from a prominent family in Saint-Malo. The couple's

The historic walled city of Saint-Malo, France. The Malouins have always had an independent outlook, and the city is famous as the home of French privateers, some pirates, and Jacques Cartier.

official marriage registry reads: "The nuptial benediction [wedding blessing] was received by Jacques Cartier, master-pilot of the port of Saincte-Malo, son of Jamet Cartier and of Geseline Jansart, and Marie Katherine des Granches, daughter of Messire Honoré des Granches, *chevalier* [knight] of our lord the king, and constable of the town and city of Saint-Malo."

Reading between the lines, historians have concluded that Cartier married a woman who was somewhat above his own social status. Cartier was only a sea pilot and the son of a sea pilot. Marie Catherine's father, Jacques des Granches, was a far more prominent man—the town's constable and *un chevalier du roi* (a knight of the king). Leacock writes, "In all probability he [des Granches] stood a few degrees higher in the social scale of the period than such plain seafaring folk as the Cartier family."

Even so, it is likely that by the time Cartier married, he was already a respected mariner who was experienced at making extended voyages. There are no definite records of any long trips he made to the New World, but the seagoing men of France were already regularly visiting Newfoundland on fishing expeditions. It is therefore likely that Cartier was on at least one such trip. Historian Marcel Trudel notes in *The Beginnings of New France*, "[A]s far as Newfoundland is concerned it would be very surprising if a Saint-Malo pilot over forty years of age had never been there." One piece of evidence that shows that Cartier had probably made his way there is that on his first official voyage of discovery, he sailed to Newfoundland directly and made landfall precisely where he wanted to go. Clearly, he knew the route well.

Cartier also stated that, as a young man, he had been on an expeditionary voyage to Brazil. Although there is no hard evidence to prove this, it is entirely possible. For one thing, he was fluent in Portuguese. Further evidence noted in Leacock's *The Mariner of Saint-Malo* consists of a few references found in the accounts of Cartier's journeys to Canada, in which he shows familiarity with plants found in Brazil. In his account of his first voyage to Canada, for instance, Cartier compares the maize (corn) of Canada to another vegetable from the South American country: "There groweth likewise a kind of [cereal] as big as peason [peas] like unto that which groweth in Bresil."

Cartier's trip to Brazil may have been one led in 1527 by the Italian explorer Giovanni da Verrazano (also spelled Verrazzano), who sailed under the flag of François I, the king of France. Verrazano's fame rests on an earlier voyage, when he explored the northeast coast of what is now the United States. His exploration took him from the site of present-day

Charleston, South Carolina, to Maine. The journey covered roughly the coastline between the Spanish colony of Florida and a Portuguese outpost on Cape Breton Island, which is now part of the Canadian province of Nova Scotia.

## A Powerful Supporter

Still, nothing is certain about Cartier's career before 1532. That year marked the start of his first documented voyage to North America, when François I decided to mount a major expedition there.

François I was a firm supporter of the new wave of exploration and enlightenment being forged by the Renaissance. Two of his trusted and influential advisers further encouraged him to fund another venture to the New World. One of these men was among the most powerful clergymen in France: Jean Le Veneur, a nobleman who ranked highly in the Catholic Church. He was the bishop, and later cardinal, of Saint-Malo and the abbot of a famous abbey, Mont St. Michel. Le Veneur introduced Cartier (who was a relative of Le Veneur's treasurer) to the king and recommended him as a leader for the voyage.

Le Veneur assured François that Cartier's experiences sailing to Brazil and Newfoundland were sufficient to lead ships of discovery. In fact, Le Veneur was so confident in Cartier's abilities that he promised to reach into his own pocket to help pay for the trip. As recorded in Trudel's *The Beginnings of New France*, he stated that "if the King would consent to entrust this mission to Jacques Cartier," the clergyman himself would "provide chaplains and contribute to the cost of these voyages of discovery from his own resources."

Cartier's other chief supporter was the Count of Charni and Lord of Brion, Philippe de Chabot. Brion, as he was known, was a childhood friend of the king, a naval admiral, and a favorite at François's court. With Brion's approval, François authorized the trip and gave Cartier enough funding to outfit two ships of 60 tons each (54 metric tons).

Another goal of expeditions at this time was missionary work: converting the people of the New World to Christianity. Missionary work was apparently not of major importance on Cartier's journey. No clear mention is made of that goal in surviving documents, although at least one priest traveled with Cartier.

Instead, perhaps the most important of the formally stated reasons for the expedition was to search for a passage through or around North America to Asia. The voyages of the Spaniards to the regions around Florida, and the explorations of Verrazano along the American mid-Atlantic coast, had shown that solid land existed between Florida and what was eventually to be called Nova Scotia. But the region farther north still held the promise of a route to the Pacific. Historian W.J. Eccles writes in *The French in North America*, "This, therefore, was the route Jacques Cartier was ordered to take."

Cartier had another order as well: to seek treasure. According to Trudel, on order from the king the explorer was "to voyage to that realm of the *Terres Neufves* [New World] to discover certain isles and countries where it is said there must be great quantities of gold and other riches."

And so Cartier's first major voyage began.

# The First Voyage Begins

It was not particularly easy for Cartier to assemble his crew, ships, and supplies. He ran up against resistance to the journey from many of the merchants and fishermen of Saint-Malo. It is possible that they wanted to hold him back and thus guard the exact locations of their fishing grounds in the New World. Luckily, Cartier had good connections with the royal court and he was able to prepare for the journey by the spring of 1534.

When everything was ready, Cartier and his crew assembled in the church in Saint-Malo to receive a blessing. The group also had, of course, the best wishes of the French court. Leacock writes, "Before leaving their anchorage, the commander, the sailing-masters, and the men took an oath, administered by Charles de Mouy, vice admiral of France, that they would behave themselves truly and faithfully in the service of the Most Christian King."

# Crossing the Atlantic

The expedition set sail from Saint-Malo on April 20, 1534. Cartier was in charge of a crew of 61 men and two ships (each weighing about 60 tons), with a sailing master for each ship. The journey encountered good weather, and the ships crossed the Atlantic in only 20 days, covering a distance of a little over 2,000 nautical miles—roughly 100 nautical miles per day. (A nautical mile is equal to 1.15 miles on land.) This was a speedy trip in those days.

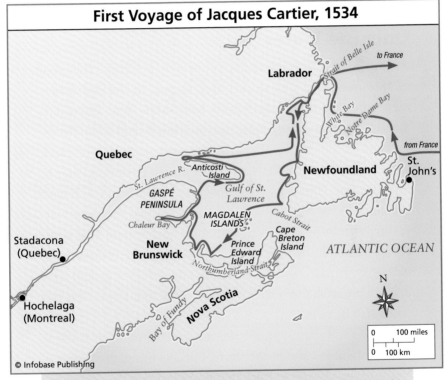

**First Voyage of Jacques Cartier, 1534**

© Infobase Publishing

By the time he was commissioned to sail to the New World in search of the Northwest Passage to Asia, it is suspected that Cartier had already gained seafaring experience by traveling to Newfoundland and Brazil. After leaving Saint-Malo with two ships, Cartier and his crew reached Newfoundland in 20 days and explored the Gulf of St. Lawrence.

Cartier and his crew made landfall on the east coast of Newfoundland, at a spot that French fishermen called *Cap Bonne Viste* (now known as Cape Bonavista). The coastline in that region is rocky and forbidding. Indeed, when Cartier and his men reached the cape in early June, the coast was still blocked with ice.

Fortunately, there were other nearby harbors that could provide shelter. Cartier's ships were able to anchor in the harbor of St. Catherine (now Catalina), where they stayed for 10 days to wait out the ice. During that time, Cartier and his crew were kept busy making needed repairs to the ships.

## Only the Water

At this point, Cartier was not yet in new territory. The coast of Newfoundland was already well known to the cod fishermen who ventured there from Saint-Malo and elsewhere. These fishermen came ashore only minimally and when necessary. At various times, they had created a scattering of crude settlements along the Newfoundland shores. Historian Peter N. Moogk comments in *La Nouvelle France: the Making of French Canada*, "From the 1490s European fishermen had been harvesting Newfoundland cod, and some [fishermen] had come ashore to obtain fresh water and firewood." The firewood was necessary, in part, because sometimes the fish they caught were dried to preserve the catch for the trip back to Europe. (The fish could also be salted.)

The fishermen typically did not go farther toward setting up a permanent spot on the shore. For one thing, the forests of Newfoundland were so thick that it was thought they could not be entered. Also, the waters were so abundant with resources that the fishermen had little need to take advantage of what was on land. As a result, they knew the coastlines well, but they made virtually no explorations inland. Historian Samuel Edward Dawson notes in *The Saint Lawrence*, "It is, of course, possible that some sailor, more curious than the rest, may have penetrated further [than the coast]; but, if so, not a vestige [trace] of his enterprise has come down to our day."

This lack of interest in exploring the land is, perhaps, not too surprising. Sailors of the time commonly believed that the land of the New World was filled with demons and monsters. To explore too far inland was a terrifying idea. "[W]oe to the sailor or the fisherman who ventured alone into the haunted woods," wrote Francis Parkman in *The Parkman Reader*.

## Birds and Polar Bears

Cartier was more interested in the land, and he was willing to go slowly, observe closely, and take careful notes and sketches. After the ships left the harbor of St. Catherine, they headed north along the coast. There the French explorers encountered the first of the abundant wildlife they would find in Canada.

They made one early stop at an island off Newfoundland called Îles-aux-Oiseaux ("Island of Birds," which today is called Funk Island). The crew had to cut through thick ice in longboats, powered by oarsmen, in order to reach the island. Once there, in just a few days Cartier's crew slaughtered about 1,000 birds to dry and salt for future food needs. Most of the birds killed were great auks, a species that later was hunted into extinction. Cartier and his men also spotted a polar bear swimming in the water, "as large as any cow and as white as a swan," writes Leacock. They chased the animal in their longboats and killed it for food, finding its meat very tender and similar to that of a young cow.

Cartier did not have to go north from St. Catherine. He also could have gone south to get around the huge island. North or south would have taken him to the large gulf to the west that is now called the Gulf of St. Lawrence. It is clear, however, that Cartier did not even know about the southern entrance to the gulf. Judging by the records he kept, the pilot knew only about

## AN OBSERVANT NAVIGATOR

According to Samuel Edward Dawson in *The Saint Lawrence: Its Basin and Border-Lands*, accounts of Cartier's various voyages were published during or shortly after his lifetime. Some scholars, however, have questioned the truth of the information in these books. They have suggested that other, more skilled writers may have used Cartier's logbooks to produce smoother and fuller documents. Others disagree.

For example, Dawson makes note of a book that refers to Cartier in the third person: "[T]here shows out from time to time in [the author's] inexperienced effort an indication that the commander of the expedition is the narrator. The style is that of a man unaccustomed to write, excepting in the technical and abrupt manner of a sailor's log. It is a sailor's style, abounding in nautical expressions. The language is Breton French [Cartier's native tongue], with technical locutions, and the grammar and spelling are very incorrect," even when taking into account the changing grammar and spelling of the time.

In any case, Dawson notes, it is for the most part accurate. He further comments, "Cartier was an observant navigator, and records all the dangers to ships in [the region].... All his distances and directions are in the main correct and his descriptions are clear and accurate."

the northern route, which led through a passage then called the Baie des Châteaux. This passage is today known as the Strait of Belle Isle, for the island at its easternmost point.

## Northward and into the Gulf

So north he went, around the northern tip of Newfoundland. While sailing through the strait, Cartier skirted the coast of

Labrador, which is on the mainland. The ships then entered the large gulf. Cartier knew about this gulf, so he was still not yet in unknown territory, and fishermen had already named a number of important landmarks there. In fact, Dawson notes, "By 1534, when Jacques Cartier first appeared in the history of discovery, the whole Atlantic seaboard of the Dominion of Canada had been explored."

Still, there were many harbors and islands that had not yet been assigned names by the French fishermen. Cartier took note of various geographical features and freely gave them names. Among the things he named were Île ("island," in French) Sainte-Catherine; Toutes-Isles; Havre ("harbor") Saint-Antoine; Havre Saint-Servan; and Rivière ("river") Saint-Jacques. Not all of these names have survived into modern times; some have been replaced by English names or names taken from North American tribal terms.

As he went, Cartier also formally claimed possession of the land. He did this by planting huge crosses hung with images of the fleur-de-lis, a representation of a lily that was the official symbol of the royalty of France.

On June 10, the ships dropped anchor in the harbor of Brest (now called Old Fort Bay), on the northern coast of the Gulf of St. Lawrence. The French fishing fleet already knew this spot. Here, Cartier and his men resupplied their ships with wood and water. The explorers then left both ships anchored in place and continued west using their longboats, smaller boats powered by oarsmen.

They came across many small islands and what appeared to be the mouth of a great river sweeping down from the interior. As the boats sat by the mouth of this river, a fishing vessel appeared. It came from the French port of La Rochelle and was now trying to find Brest, which it had sailed past and missed in the dark.

Because he had carefully noted his path, Cartier was able to supply the information the fishermen needed to navigate safely back down the coast to Brest. This ship and the men aboard it were the last traces of European life that Cartier and his crew would meet for the rest of the voyage. From this point on, they saw no other Europeans until their return to Saint-Malo.

## Entering New Territory

Cartier and his men pressed on to the west, reaching a harbor so pleasant that Cartier declared it to be one of the finest in the world. He seems to have liked it so much that he named it after himself, calling it Havre Jacques-Cartier, or Jacques Cartier Harbor. This was probably what is today called Cumberland Harbor.

Bad winds and weather forced Cartier to give up his westward direction and turn back to rejoin his ships. They got back to the ships at Brest on June 14. Cartier was pleased and grateful for a safe return, and he asked that a Catholic mass be sung.

The explorer did not think much of the land he had seen along the north shore of Newfoundland. For one thing, the soil seemed remarkably barren. As quoted by historian Leacock, Cartier noted that, although there were plenty of harbors, "In all the north land, I did not see a cartload of good earth. To be short, I believe that this was the land that God allotted to [the murdering biblical figure] Cain."

When the weather improved, Cartier continued on his journey. This time he headed south, following the west coast of Newfoundland. At some point on this leg of the journey, the expedition entered waters that had never before been explored by Europeans. "From that moment, Cartier was entering the unknown; the voyage of discovery had begun," writes historian Trudel.

About 60 miles (100 kilometers) along, still following the west coast of Newfoundland, Cartier found a point of land that is now called Point Rich. Because of its appearance, he named the formation Cap-Double (Double Cape). From this point he headed southwest, across the open water of the gulf.

To the east, Cartier could see what is today known as Cabot Strait. This is the stretch of water between the southwestern tip of Newfoundland and Cape Breton Island. Cabot Strait is the southern entrance from the Atlantic into the Gulf of St. Lawrence, and it is also the widest. But Cartier did not see that it was a channel through which he could navigate. Instead of entering it—which would have taken him completely around Newfoundland—he continued to the southwest.

By late June, the expedition had reached the Magdalen Islands, a group of small islands in the gulf. Cartier thought that these islands were the beginning of the mainland. He named the northernmost of these islands Île de Brion (Brion Island), after his patron, Philippe de Chabot, the Seigneur de Brion.

Cartier found these islands very hospitable, unlike the rocky and barren parts of Newfoundland he had seen. For instance, he found on Brion Island many kinds of trees that he recognized, including cedar, pine, yew, white elm, ash, and willow, as well as some that he did not know. Where the land was clear of trees, it was fertile, with abundant wild gooseberries, peas, strawberries, raspberries, and corn. Moreover, the climate was good, and there were doves, pigeons, and many other kinds of birds. Leacock notes that Cartier exclaimed over what he saw, declaring, "One acre of this land is worth more than all the New Land [Newfoundland]."

These islands, so lush with vegetation, were a welcome sight after the inhospitable land Cartier had seen elsewhere. Historian Dawson describes one island recorded by Cartier:

> There was a sandy beach all round it, it was full of fine trees, prairies, fields of wild corn, and of peas in flower as thick and as fine as any he ever saw in Bretagne [Brittany], and in appearance as if they had been sown. There were in abundance gooseberries, strawberries, and Provence

roses; parsley and other plants pleasant to smell. Brion Island does not seem such a paradise in the present day, but to Cartier, who had been coasting along Labrador and northern Newfoundland, it was delightful by contrast.

## "The Fairest Land"

The French explorer continued south, passing to the west of the Magdalen Islands. He then continued southwest and came in sight of a large island, now the Canadian province of Prince Edward Island. Cartier did not realize that this land was, in fact, an island separate from the mainland (which is now called New Brunswick).

From Prince Edward Island, Cartier continued on until the New Brunswick coast was in sight. He crossed what is now called the Northumberland Strait, which separates Prince Edward Island from the mainland. Cartier thought that this strait was just a large bay and did not explore it. Instead he chose to continue northwest, following the outline of the New Brunswick coast and exploring the series of bays along it. Each was an opening into the mainland that held the promise of being the much-sought passage to Asia. Each one grew narrower, however, as the explorers advanced into it and proved disappointing.

The ships made slow progress because of strong winds coming in from the outer gulf. Thick mist and fog often covered them. Nonetheless, historian Leacock says that Cartier was delighted with what he saw along the New Brunswick coast, noting: "It is the fairest land, that may possibly be seen, full of goodly meadows and trees."

Cartier named the largest bay he found on the New Brunswick coast the Baie des Chaleurs (Chaleur Bay or "Bay of Warmth"), because of the good weather he encountered there. The explorer had especially high hopes that it might be the passage to Asia. In this spirit, he named the southern tip of

During his journey through the Gulf of St. Lawrence, Cartier discovered many different bays, peninsulas, and capes, in the area. Cartier began naming many of them, including Baie de Gaspé (Gaspé Bay), a place where he and his men found sanctuary from rough seas and met with the Iroquois, the indigenous group of the area *(above)*.

the bay Cap d'Espérance ("Cape of Hope"). As quoted by Trudel, Cartier wrote, "[B]ecause of the depth and tide marks and changing nature of the land, we had hope of finding the passage there." But it was only the mouth of another small river. Despite a careful investigation, Cartier had to sadly conclude that he had not yet found a passage.

Chaleur Bay partially separates a large land formation, the Gaspé Peninsula, from the rest of New Brunswick. On July 16, near the northeastern tip of the peninsula, Cartier sailed into another hospitable bay, now called Baie de Gaspé (Gaspé Bay).

He and his group stayed there until late in the month, waiting out the stormy weather that was again slowing their progress. Leacock writes that the explorers saw "so dark a sky and so violent a storm raging over the Gulf that not even the daring seamen of Saint-Malo thought it wise to venture out." It was here, in Chaleur Bay and Gaspé Bay, that Cartier had two momentous encounters: his first significant meetings with North American Indians.

# Exploring
# New Territory

EARLIER, CARTIER'S GROUP HAD BRIEFLY SIGHTED THE REGION'S inhabitants. In mid-June, for instance, they saw a group of North American Indians who seemed to be hunting seals. This was probably a group of Beothuk, members of a Newfoundland tribe that is now extinct. The Beothuk were known for painting their bodies, clothes, and belongings with red ocher. One historical theory is that this habit was the origin of the outdated phrase "Red Indians."

In early July, the French explorers also spotted a man running along the shore of Prince Edward Island making signs with his hands as if he wanted to meet with them. By the time the explorers got ashore, however, he had fled. They left a knife and some cloth for him, tied to a stick set in the sand.

## A Meeting

Still, these were brief encounters. Cartier's first significant meeting with the people of the St. Lawrence region came on July 7 in

Chaleur Bay, when he and his crew encountered a large fishing party of an estimated 200 canoes.

This meeting was not the very first encounter between the North American native peoples and Europeans. It is known, for instance, that European fishermen had traded with the people of this region before. Nonetheless, it is a significant event because it was the first *documented* meeting between Europeans and North American Indians of the Gulf of St. Lawrence.

This party was part of a tribe called the Micmac (also sometimes spelled Miqmak), which in turn was part of the huge Algonquin Nation. The Micmac clearly already had some contact with Europeans, because the groups that met Cartier already knew that the Frenchman might be interested in trading for furs. They demonstrated this by holding up their furs on sticks while still a distance away. (Since there was no interpreter, the groups could not speak to each other except in crude sign language.) The French were greatly outnumbered and, frightened, they tried to slip away. The Micmac persisted and Cartier ordered his men to fire muskets over their heads.

## Offering Food and Gifts

When the Micmac heard the firing muskets they scattered, but the following day they came back and made their friendly intentions clear. As a result, they were able to trade with the French. The explorers gave the Micmac knives, beads, and other small objects. In return the Micmac gave the French explorers furs.

The Micmac were so eager to trade that they even traded away the furs they were wearing. Cartier wrote, as noted by Leacock, "They gave us whatsoever they had, not keeping anything, so that they were constrained to go back again naked, and made us signs that the next day they would come again and bring more skins with them."

Hundreds of others from the Micmac village came to see the Frenchmen. They arrived in canoes and on the shore, and were very friendly, giving the explorers pieces of cooked meat and other food. According to Leacock, they were extremely respectful. He writes, "Their manner was as of those offering food to the gods who have descended from above."

The Micmac indicated in other ways that they regarded the Europeans as semi-godlike. For example, the women from the village stroked the explorers with their hands and then lifted their clasped hands to the sky, as if expressing joy. The Micmac on the shore also sang and danced for the explorers. Cartier responded by passing out iron knives, glass beads, combs, tin bells, and other small articles as gifts to them.

## Donnacona's Group

Cartier's men had an even more significant encounter in July 1534, one that would have far-reaching effects. This was with another group of North American Indians whom they met in Gaspé Bay. They came, as Cartier later learned, from a village called Stadacona, upstream on the St. Lawrence River. They were in Gaspé Bay on an annual fishing expedition. This group was part of a tribe that is now usually called the St. Lawrence Iroquois. Their leader was a chief named Donnacona, with whom Cartier would form a history-making relationship.

Cartier wanted to befriend Donnacona, and Donnacona was willing, but the explorer also angered the chief. On July 24, at a spot called Penouille Point, the French explorer set up a 30-foot (9-meter) wooden cross with a shield adorned with three French fleur-de-lis. The cross was inscribed *Vive le Roi de France* ("Long live the king of France").

The raising of the cross upset Donnacona, who came out to the French ships in a canoe in the company of his brother and three of his sons. The chief made a long, angry speech. Cartier wrote, as reported by historian Trudel, that the chief began his speech by "pointing to the cross and making the sign of the cross with two fingers; then he pointed to the land all around

The initial meeting between Cartier and Donnacona, the local Iroquois chief, was tense due to distrust and suspicion. Donnacona believed that Cartier, who had erected a large cross with French words on one of the nearby beaches, was only there to place the area under French rule. Cartier did his best to convince the tribal leader that the French were not interested in land, and even resorted to trickery in order to gain Donnacona's confidence.

us, as if to say that all the land was his, and that we should not have planted the cross without his leave [permission]."

The French still had no interpreter, so they could not understand Donnacona perfectly, but they got the general idea. Cartier tried to convince the Iroquois chief that the cross was

## OBSERVING THE NORTH AMERICAN INDIANS OF ST. LAWRENCE

Among Cartier's written accounts of his travels are several close observations of the North American Indians he encountered. One of his many comments on the subject concerned how strange he considered their practice of bathing daily in streams. Europeans at the time generally thought that bathing more than once a year was unhealthy. In *The Mariner of St. Malo*, Stephen Leacock notes Cartier's reaction upon first meeting Donnacona's group of St. Lawrence Iroquois:

> They are men of an indifferent good stature and bigness, but wild and unruly. They wear their hair tied on the top like a wreath of hay and put a wooden pin within it, or any other such thing instead of a nail, and with them they bind certain birds' feathers. They are clothed with beasts' skins as well the men as women, but that the women go somewhat straighter and closer in their garments than the men do, with their waists girded. They paint themselves with certain roan colours [reddish brown, brown, or black speckled with white or gray].
>
> Their boats are made with the bark of birch trees, with . . . which they fish and take great store of seals, and, as far as we could understand since our coming thither, that is not their habitation, but they come from the mainland out of hotter countries to catch the said seals and other necessaries for their living.

simply a navigational aid for future explorers, but Donnacona seems to have had his doubts. Leacock writes that the chief and the other Iroquois were wary with good reason, because "they rightly saw in the erection of the cross the advancing shadow of the rule of the white man."

Soon after, just as the Frenchmen were preparing to leave and continue their explorations, Cartier tricked Donnacona. He pretended that he wanted to offer the Iroquois chief an ax in exchange for a fur. When Donnacona paddled near the ship, the pilot ordered his sailors to seize the canoe. The chief was then forced to go aboard the ship, along with his two sons and other Iroquois who were accompanying him.

Naturally, the chief was outraged, but Cartier was able to smooth over the bad feelings. He managed to convince Donnacona that the cross was just an insignificant landmark to aid in navigation for future sailors. He also provided a feast for Donnacona. This seems to have worked well. Cartier was so convincing that he persuaded the Iroquois chief to let his two sons, Domagaya and Taignoagny, sail away with him. Cartier wanted to do this because the French needed to train interpreters, and the young men seemed willing.

Cartier promised to bring the two back in a year. Donnacona accepted this, and agreed to let his sons accompany the Frenchman. The two groups then held another feast, after which the explorers left Gaspé Bay with Donnacona's sons.

## Turning Back

At this point Cartier and his ships could have rounded the tip of the Gaspé Peninsula and turned west. If they had, the explorer would have discovered the mouth of the St. Lawrence River on this, his first voyage. Instead he chose to go northeast, crossing what is now Honguedo Strait, and on July 29 he came in sight of a large island with a rocky, dangerous coast. He named this land L'Assumption.

Cartier neglected to thoroughly explore an isle he called L' Assumption and missed the mouth of the St. Lawrence River. Later renamed Anticosti, the island received many more unwilling visitors, as the treacherous waters in the area caused as many as 400 shipwrecks in less than 400 years. Today, almost every household on Anticosti Island owns pieces of valuable china, porcelain, or Spanish-silver candlesticks salvaged from these disastrous voyages.

At this point, he did not realize it was an island. He thought the land was a peninsula extending from the mainland. Today, this island is called Anticosti Island. Its name is a corruption of the Micmac name for it, Natiscotec. Cartier's expedition sailed east along its southern edge and rounded its easternmost point.

The Frenchman named this point Cap St. Louis. The expedition then turned west and followed the island's north coast, at the beginning of what is now called Jacques-Cartier Passage. Cartier did not complete a full trip around Anticosti Island. If he had, he would have discovered that Jacques-Cartier Passage completely separated the island from the mainland.

Cartier decided not to continue much farther. The journey was growing increasingly slow and dangerous. As the passage grew narrow, his ships encountered powerful tides and strange, treacherous currents. Furthermore, the wind was now coming from the west, which meant that the ships had to battle it head-on. Worst of all was the season. Autumn was approaching and with it, Cartier knew, would come storms.

Still, the explorer did not give up right away. He tried to take a couple of longboats manned by rowers farther along the passage, but the tides and the winds were too strong for them. Even with double the usual number of men rowing in each boat, it was impossible to make progress.

The party then landed on Anticosti and a small group tried to make progress westward on foot. This party eventually reached the island's western tip. Nonetheless, Cartier realized that none of his vessels could go any farther that year.

As a result, the explorer made the decision to return to France. It was a wise evaluation of the situation. The trip had always been planned as one of simple exploration, and the crew did not have enough supplies to last through a winter. "Cartier called together his sailing-master, pilots, and mates to discuss what had to be done," wrote Leacock. "They agreed that the contrary winds forbade further exploration. The season was already late; the coast of France was far away; within a few weeks the great gales of the equinox would be upon them."

And so Cartier turned back to the east. Now his ships were running with the powerful westerly winds blowing behind them, and they made swift progress. By August 9, they reached the port of Blanc Sablon in the Strait of Belle Isle. It was the same passage through which Cartier and his ships had passed on their way west in the spring. Blanc Sablon (the name means "fine, white sand") is on the mainland, in what is now the province of Quebec. The crew spent a few days there, preparing the ships for the long sea voyage ahead of them.

The ships left for France on August 15. For Cartier, it was a promising day to start a voyage. August 15 is the Feast of the Assumption of Our Lady, an important date in the Catholic calendar. According to Leacock, Cartier wrote,

> After … we had heard service, we altogether departed from the port of Blanc Sablon, and with a happy and prosperous weather we came into the middle of the sea that is between Newfoundland and Brittany, in which place we were tossed and turmoiled three days long with great storms and windy tempests coming from the east, which with the aid and assistance of God we suffered; then we had fair weather, and upon the fifth day of September, in the said year, we came to the port of St.-Malo whence we departed.

## Back in France

Cartier's safe return to France was greeted with thanks and appreciation. François, his royal sponsor, considered the voyage to be overall a great success. It was true, however, that in many ways the explorer did not succeed. He had not found gold, diamonds, or the fabled passage to Asia. Furthermore, as later explorers realized, his knowledge of the land and waters he had explored was severely limited. For example, he failed to notice the passage between Newfoundland and Cape Breton Island, which would have provided a second entrance from the sea to the gulf. Also, he thought the Magdalen Islands were part of the mainland, and he missed the entry to the St. Lawrence River.

On the other hand, Cartier had accomplished many important tasks. He had made contact and begun a crucial alliance with a tribe of North American Indians. He also brought back reports of greatly abundant natural resources, a prospect that pleased the king. And, despite his errors, he was the first European to explore an "inland sea"—the Gulf of St. Lawrence—and to catch a glimpse of what lay beyond it. (It is possible that earlier Europeans, such as John Cabot or the Portuguese explorer João Alvares Fagundes, had seen it before him, but these speculations have never been proven.)

Furthermore, Cartier had returned with Donnacona's two sons, who would learn French and thus become valuable interpreters. The Iroquois whetted the king's appetite for further exploration by relating tantalizing stories about the Kingdom of Saguenay, a fabulous land of gold that lay inland. (It is likely that the "gold" Domagaya and Taignoagny were talking about was in fact raw copper, brought to the St. Lawrence Valley by other tribes who lived in the region around Lake Superior.)

All of Cartier's successes convinced François that more exploration of the New World was clearly necessary. Trudel writes:

> The discovery of an inland sea, a visit to a new country, an alliance with natives from the west, a hypothetical passage that might open the way to further exploration, the possibility of commercial gain; all this was enough to justify a second attempt, the more so since Cartier had brought home two natives who, with their initiation in the French language, were to stimulate interest in this new venture.

The king was encouraged to immediately begin efforts, on a much larger scale, to mount a second expedition.

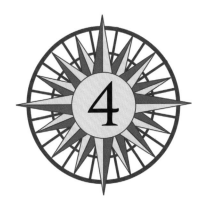

# The Second Voyage Begins

CARTIER WASTED NO TIME IN MOUNTING HIS SECOND VOYAGE. This expedition is generally considered to be the high point of Cartier's career. Leacock calls it "the exploit on which his title to fame chiefly rests."

By late October 1534, less than two months after the explorer's return from the New World, he received a formal commission to mount this second expedition. His official title for the journey was "Captain and Pilot of the King." This voyage was, as the royal commission stated, "completion of the navigation in the lands beyond the *Terres Neufves* whose discovery [Cartier had] already begun," notes Trudel.

This voyage was on a much grander scale. On his first trip, Cartier had taken only two ships and 61 men. Now he was allotted three ships that were much larger than his earlier ones, a crew of some 110, and enough supplies to last 15 months.

As with his first voyage, Cartier had some difficulty in supplying and manning his ships. The merchants and fishermen of

Saint-Malo again proved resistant to a voyage, funded by the king, to explore terrain they felt was theirs. However, Cartier's connections again proved useful—particularly Chabot—and eventually enough men and supplies were found. Of the men who sailed, the names of 84 were recorded for history. It appears that some of them were criminals taken from the jails of France, perhaps because not enough regular sailors could be found.

## Cartier's Relatives

Cartier himself was the captain and pilot aboard the expedition's flagship, *La Grande Hermine*. At 120 tons (108 metric tons), it was twice the size of either of the ships he had taken for the first voyage. The shipmaster of *La Grande Hermine*, Cartier's assistant, was Thomas Fromont. Among those also on board this main ship, in addition to the regular crew, were Claude de Pontbriand, the son of a nobleman, the Seigneur de Montréal; Jehan Poullet, who is thought to have written an account of the voyage; and several other gentlemen.

The second ship, *La Petite Hermine,* was 60 tons (54 metric tons). Guillaume Le Marié was the shipmaster, under the command of Macé Jalobert, Cartier's brother-in-law. And the third ship, smaller still, was *L'Émérillon*, commanded by Captain Guillaume Le Breton Bastille.

Jalobert was not Cartier's only relative on the expedition. The navigator of *L'Émérillon*, Jacques Maingart, was also related, as were several other gentlemen on board, including Étienne Noël, a nephew, Antoine des Granches, and three other Maingarts. Altogether, about a dozen Cartier relatives, either by blood or by marriage, took part in the adventure.

## Other Passengers

Donnacona's sons, Domagaya and Taignoagny, also returned to the New World on this second voyage. During their eight

Cartier returned to France with two natives (sons of the Iroquois chief, Donnacona) and reports of the available natural resources in the New World. Although Cartier did not find the fabled Northwest Passage, King François I believed the reports had potential and needed further exploration. Cartier was immediately granted funds for a second voyage, one that would allow him three large ships and almost double the amount of men. *La Grande Hermine (above)*, his flagship vessel, would lead the way back to North America.

and a half months in France, they had learned French well and were ready to serve as interpreters.

It is unclear whether any priests accompanied Cartier. It is likely that chaplains would have been part of a large expedition

## A NEW KIND OF PEOPLE

As the earliest European explorers returned with tales of their adventures, people were amazed at what they said about the native inhabitants of North America. In particular, they marveled at the existence of a vast group of people to whom known religions meant nothing. Historian Peter N. Moogk writes:

> Europeans had wondered if these beings were humans like themselves with immortal souls and the power of reason. The Bible and ancient histories were assumed to be comprehensive accounts of human existence, yet here was a hitherto-unacknowledged fourth continent with people not described by the authoritative works.

The matter was finally settled by decrees from the Pope, issued in 1495 and 1512. They asserted that North America's native peoples were, indeed, the children of Adam and Eve, and were therefore humans. Nonetheless, when Cartier returned from his first journey with a pair of Iroquois brothers, they were still odd and fascinating marvels in the Europeans' eyes. One of the explorer's purposes in bringing them to Europe was to let them learn French and so become useful interpreters. But another reason was simply to show them off to the royalty of France as exotic curiosities.

such as this one. Also, it seems that religious ceremonies were performed on the voyage, since there are references to such ceremonies in accounts of the trip. On the other hand, when Donnacona and his people later asked for baptism, after Cartier had reached their land, Cartier replied that he expected to bring priests with him on another voyage, and that they would be able to perform this ceremony.

In any case, there is not yet any positive proof concerning priests on the voyage. The official tallies of the ships' crews list two names preceded by the word *dom*. This may have indicated that they were priests, but they may also have been simply abbreviations for the first name "Dominique." It is also possible that the men listed as "dom" were priests who died en route.

## A Stormy Crossing

In mid-May 1535, Cartier and his crew assembled in the cathedral at Saint-Malo to confess their sins and receive the blessing and absolution of the town's bishop. They sailed from the port on May 19. It was a much more difficult crossing than before. Parkman writes, "The dingy walls of the rude old seaport, and the white rocks that line the neighboring shores of Brittany, faded from their sight, and soon they were tossing in a furious tempest." After a week of good weather, storms separated the vessels. Dawson notes, "He [Cartier] had five weeks of the worst weather the North Atlantic could produce: contrary wind, thick fog, and heavy storms, so that the ships parted company and did not see each other until they arrived at the rendezvous at Blanc Sablon."

Cartier reached this rendezvous point on July 15, but the other ships did not all arrive until July 26. After refitting the vessels and taking on fresh water—tasks that took three days—the expedition was ready to continue. Historian Trudel comments, "Cartier had only one immediate preoccupation, and that was to take up his investigations where he had left them the previous year."

## On to "Canada"

This time, the expedition followed the coast of Labrador westward through the strait now named for Cartier, with Anticosti Island to the south. This was the same route, only in reverse, that he had taken on his way home from the first voyage. Cartier described this coast as dangerous and rocky. His ships could travel only slowly, and only in the daylight. He searched, mainly with no luck, for good harbors.

Along the way, Domagaya and Taignoagny recognized familiar territory and, because they now spoke French, they could communicate their knowledge to Cartier. They cleared up one important point for the explorer: Anticosti was an island, not part of the mainland.

Late in July the coast changed, becoming flat and sandy, and Cartier began to recognize points of land he had seen before. In familiar waters again, he was able to resume sailing at night. Early in August the wind turned against the ships and he was forced to take refuge in a small harbor he called Havre St. Nicholas. While waiting, he put up another cross.

The sons of Donnacona told Cartier that the water route west from the Gaspé Peninsula was the way to what they called "Canada." Cartier's mention of this in his logbook, on August 13, 1535, is the first known written record of that word. Cartier took it to mean all the land around, although it later became clear that it was simply the Iroquois word for *village*. Domagaya and Taignoagny were pointing the way to their home.

On August 10, Cartier chose a name for a local land feature that would prove to be significant. He finally found an excellent bay, which he named St. Laurent. (This bay is now called Sainte-Geneviève.) Trudel quotes Cartier's account: "[W]e

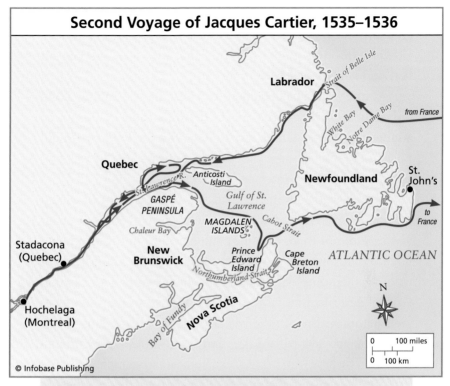

## Second Voyage of Jacques Cartier, 1535–1536

On his second voyage, Cartier decided not to start at the same location of his first expedition, instead choosing to move backwards along the original route. With the help of the two Iroquois on his crew, Cartier realized that Anticosti was not a peninsula, but an island near the mouth of the St. Lawrence River. From there, Cartier was able to travel inland to Canada for the first time.

found a large and very beautiful bay, full of islands and good entrances." He gave the bay this name because he entered it on the day of the Catholic calendar dedicated to St. Lawrence. Later mapmakers eventually made the name famous, giving it to a great river, the gulf into which it empties, and the surrounding valley.

The explorer continued to the mouth of what proved to be that river. Zigzagging from one shore of the broad river to another, in order to avoid missing any possible opening, he found that it gradually narrowed. The water, meanwhile, was gradually becoming fresher and less salty. According to Trudel, Cartier's Iroquois guides told him that the river "goes so far that no man has ever been to the end."

Cartier was not delighted to realize he was sailing along a river. A freshwater river meant that this route could not be a saltwater passage all the way to Asia. But the Frenchman did not want to return home with no new findings, and he was prepared to spend the winter, so he kept going.

Travel was slow and painstaking at this point. Winds and fog made vision poor and the situation dangerous. Cartier was careful not to let the ships run aground in this unknown territory. Along the way the crew spotted an abundance of wildlife, including beluga whales, which Dawson writes that Cartier described as "a kind of fish which no man had ever seen before or heard of . . . as large as porpoises, and [with] no sword [like swordfishes]. . . . white as snow, and without a spot."

The Europeans also saw another creature that was new to them: walruses. Some of the crew thought they resembled fish-shaped horses, while Cartier described them as "beasts like large oxen, which had two tusks in their mouths like elephants."

## Up the River

One of the landmarks they passed was the mouth of a deep and rapid river that emptied into the St. Lawrence from the northwest. Domagaya and Taignoagny told the Frenchmen that this was the route to the kingdom of Saguenay, where gold was to be found. Cartier accordingly named it the Saguenay River.

Continuing up the St. Lawrence, Cartier noted high mountains of bare rock on either side of the river. Huge trees seemed to grow straight out of the rock. Cartier judged that they would be big enough to make masts for large ships.

Six days after spotting the Saguenay River, on September 7, the expedition reached a group of 14 islands in the St. Lawrence. Since Domagaya and Taignoagny said they marked the beginning of "Canada," some historians consider the date to be Cartier's arrival in Canada.

Cartier named the largest of these the Ile de Bacchus, because of the many grape vines growing wild there. (Bacchus was the Roman god of wine.) He later renamed it Ile d'Orléans in honor of the Duke of Orléans, who was a son of François I. It still has that name today, and is a suburb of present-day Quebec City.

Cartier spotted North American Indians there and went ashore to meet them, but at first they fled. When the sons of Donnacona appeared in European clothes and spoke, the Iroquois returned. They then brought gifts of eels, corn, and melons so that a feast could be held.

The next day brought Cartier nearer to the village of Stadacona, Donnacona's home. (This spot is near the site of present-day Quebec City.) Donnacona came out by canoe to the French ships, accompanied by a dozen more canoes, to be reunited with his sons. He again gave a lengthy speech, with many gestures, but this time the speech was a happy one. Cartier responded by presenting him with gifts of food and drink. The French crew then accompanied Donnacona to a spot near the village, where they had a short celebration.

Though outwardly friendly, the Iroquois were wary of the visitors. This was shown at first by the fact that they did not invite them to the village of Stadacona itself, and they hid the village's women in the woods. More serious was the fact that the chief and his sons tried to talk Cartier out of going farther upriver to the village of Hochelaga, which was inhabited by another tribe that was part of the Iroquois Nation but probably of a different historical background. (The Stadacona were probably originally Mohawks, while the Hochelaga were probably Onondaga.)

The tribe told Cartier that there was nothing of value upstream. This was because Donnacona wanted to maintain a monopoly on future trade in the St. Lawrence Valley, and so he sought to prevent the Frenchmen from befriending people living upstream. Writes Eccles:

> The French were to encounter opposition from the Indians for the same reason again and again during the next

## FRIGHTENING THE FRENCHMEN

When Donnacona and his sons could not persuade Cartier to give up his plan of continuing up the river to Hochelaga, they made one last attempt. They tried to frighten the French with the supernatural. According to Leacock:

> Instead of coming near the ships, as they had done on each preceding day, the Indians secreted themselves in the woods along the shore. There they lay hid for many hours, while the French were busied with their preparations for departure. But later in the day, when the tide was running swiftly outward, the Indians in their canoes came paddling down the stream towards the ships, not, however, trying to approach them, but keeping some little distance away as if in expectation of something unusual.
> The mystery soon revealed itself. From beneath the foliage of the river bank a canoe shot into the stream. . . . The three Indians in the canoe had been carefully made up . . . to strike horror into Cartier and his companions. They were "dressed like devils, being wrapped in dog skins, white and black, their faces besmeared as black as any coals, with horns on their heads more than a yard long."
> The canoe came rushing swiftly down the stream, and floated past the ships, the "devils" who occupied the craft making no

two centuries and more. The natives of Stadacona did not want [others] to have the wondrous metal goods the French had brought, or if they were to have them, to receive them only through the medium of trade with the Iroquois of Stadacona.

The chief offered to give three small children to Cartier, as a sign of confidence, if the voyage upstream did not take place. Cartier accepted the children as an act of good faith, in exchange giving Donnacona two swords and a brass bowl.

attempt to stop, not even turning towards the ships. . . . The devil in the centre shouted a fierce harangue [angry speech] into the air. . . . The "devils," as soon as their boat was seized by [other Iroquois in canoes], fell back as if lifeless in their canoe. The assembled flotilla [group of canoes] was directed to the shore. The "devils" were lifted out rigid and lifeless and carried solemnly into the forest. . . . The French could still hear the noise of cries and incantations that broke the stillness of the woods.

After half an hour Taignoagny and Domagaya issued from among the trees. Their . . . faces simulated the religious ecstasy of men who have spoken with the gods. The caps that they had worn were now placed beneath the folds of their Indian blankets, and their clasped hands were uplifted to the autumn sky. . . . Cartier urged [Taignoagny] to explain, and the guide, still acting the part of one who bears tidings from heaven, said that the great god [had spoken] and had sent down three "spirits" in the canoe to warn Cartier that he must not try to come to Hochelaga, because there was so much ice and snow in that country that whoever went there should die.

[When Cartier was not frightened] Taignoagny asked Cartier if he had spoken with Jesus. Cartier answered no, but said that his priests had done so and that Jesus had told them that the weather would be fine. Taignoagny . . . professed a great joy at hearing this, and set off into the woods, whence he emerged presently with the whole band of Indians, singing and dancing. Their plan had failed, but they evidently thought it wiser to offer no further opposition to Cartier's journey, though all refused to go with him.

Donnacona made a further attempt to convince Cartier, but the explorer did not agree to halt his exploration.

## The Hochelaga

Cartier left his two larger ships at Stadacona, leaving some men to watch over them. He then took 50 men, the smaller ship (*L'Émérillon*), and two longboats upriver. Domagaya and Taignoagny refused to go with him, so Cartier had no interpreters on this leg of the trip.

Progress was slow. Nonetheless, the explorers were able to reach a lake—essentially an expansion of the river that was some 20 miles (32 km) wide. Cartier named this area Angelouleme. It was later renamed Lac St. Pierre (St. Peter Lake).

Along the way, Cartier saw fine land on either side of the river, full of grapevines and other vegetation, as well as abundant varieties of birds. The explorer also encountered many North American Indians. Most were friendly and eager to trade fish and other items for French goods. According to Trudel, on September 14 Cartier found a "very beautiful and pleasant fork in the waters, at a place where there is a small river and harbor with a bar."

By early October the expedition reached the Iroquois town of Hochelaga. This village, the largest he had seen so far, was near what is now Montreal. An estimated 1,000 Iroquois came to greet the Frenchmen. The site of their meeting is probably the point where the city's Jacques Cartier Bridge now stands.

The Iroquois brought the explorers ashore and led them to an open clearing in their village. Historian Parkman described how the Iroquois brought out their sick in the hopes that the Frenchman could cure them. It was as if, Cartier noted, "a god had come down to cure them."

One of these was the village chief, whose arms and legs were withered although he was only about 50 years old. He was brought with great ceremony before Cartier, who was asked to

After leaving his two ships with Chief Donnacona, Cartier continued up the St. Lawrence, in search of riches and the Northwest Passage. He soon reached a large Iroquois village at Hochelaga, where he was greeted by a group of natives. Believing these unfamiliar European travelers to be sent from their god, the members of this local tribe brought out their sick in hopes that Cartier could heal them (above).

rub his arms and legs with his own hands, apparently in the belief that this would cure the chief. Cartier rubbed the man's limbs, recited the Gospel of St. John, prayed aloud to a spell-bound audience, and passed out gifts.

## Finding Little China

While he was there, Cartier climbed a nearby mountain he named *Mont Réal* ("Mount Royal"), from which the present-day city of Montreal's name comes. From the mountaintop he could see the country in its autumn colors for miles around. He noticed mountain chains to the north and south.

Cartier's Iroquois hosts used small sticks and sign language to make it clear that there were violent rapids upstream. They also told Cartier that there was another great river, coming from the west, which led through broad lakes and rapids until it reached a freshwater sea. Now called the Ottawa River, Cartier thought this waterway was perhaps another route to Saguenay. The Iroquois said that men who wore European clothing lived along it and had metal similar to the silver of the captain's whistle and the copper of a sailor's knife handle.

Pressing on, Cartier encountered the rapids. They were just upstream from the village and were far too difficult to navigate, dropping 42 feet (13 m) in just a couple of miles. Cartier called them "the most impetuous cataract that it would be possible to see," writes Trudel. Years later, another explorer, La Salle, would jokingly give these rapids (because the route clearly did not lead to Asia) the name *Petite Chine*, or "Little China." Today, they are called the Lachine Rapids.

## Preparing for Winter

By now the season was rapidly growing late, and there was no time for more exploration. Cartier returned back down the river to Hochelaga after less than a day. He reached the village on October 4 and continued on to Stadacona, arriving there on October 11. He had been gone from Stadacona a total of three weeks.

Although Donnacona claimed to still be friendly, Cartier found that relations between the Iroquois and the men he had left behind had seriously worsened during his absence. In part, this was because Donnacona's sons had told others that the goods the French had been trading were cheap trinkets. The Iroquois were also suspicious of the Europeans' long-term plans in the area. Because of the tension, the Frenchmen who had stayed in Stadacona had built a fort to protect themselves while Cartier was away. It included a barricade and cannons taken from the ships.

Winter was approaching quickly, and Cartier decided it was too late to return to France. He tied up all three ships and gave his men the task of preparing for winter. This meant jobs such as adding a moat and drawbridge to the fort, stockpiling firewood, and preserving a season's worth of game and fish.

And so the winter began.

# Wintering
# in Stadacona

It was a long and hard winter in Stadacona. To start with, there was the weather. Stadacona's latitude is roughly the same as that of Paris. Cartier expected the weather to be similar, and the difference was a severe shock. W.J. Eccles writes that Cartier was "blissfully unaware of the length and severity of the Canadian winter, deceived by the heat of the past summer and a latitude more than two degrees south of Paris."

To make matters worse, that winter was colder than usual, even for that rugged region. The snow reached a height of 4 feet (1.2 meters) or more, and subzero winds howled across the river. From mid-November to mid-April, the French ships were completely icebound. The water froze as far upstream as Hochelaga, and its ice was as much as a fathom thick (6 feet, or 1.8 meters). All of the liquids stored in casks on the ships froze, and below deck the ice was as thick as four fingers on a sailor's hands.

Cartier, having traveled to Hochelaga and seen the impassable river rapids of the St. Lawrence, returned to Stadacona and decided to stay there for the winter. Because tensions were rising between the crew and Donnacona's tribe, a fort was built and preparations for winter included adding a moat and a drawbridge to the fortification *(above)*.

## Scurvy

As if the cold was not enough, the explorers also suffered from a terrible disease called scurvy. Scurvy is caused by a lack of vitamin C. It is often associated with sailors who don't have access to fresh fruit and vegetables at sea, but it can also affect people on land. Scurvy first causes spots on the skin, spongy gums, and bleeding from the lips, gums, nostrils, and elsewhere.

In later stages, scurvy causes depression and dementia, nausea, internal bleeding, weight loss, muscle pain, open wounds, and loss of teeth. It is often fatal.

It took a serious toll on the French camp. Out of the 110 men in the camp, fewer than 10 remained strong through the entire winter. At least 8 of them died. (Some sources say the dead totaled 25.) Their comrades could not bury the corpses in the frozen ground, so the bodies were left in snow banks until the spring. Leacock writes:

> The plague that had fallen upon them was such as none of them had ever before seen. The legs of the sufferers swelled to huge, unsightly, and livid masses of flesh. Their sinews shriveled to blackened strings, pimpled with purple clots of blood. The awful disease worked its way upwards. The arms hung hideous and useless at the side, the mouth rotted till the teeth fell from the putrid flesh. Chilled with the cold [and] fast frozen in the endless desolation of the snow, the agonized sufferers breathed their last, remote from aid, far from the love of women, and deprived of the consolations of the Church.

## A "Most Excellent" Remedy

Cartier and his crew, all of them Catholics, often turned to prayer in hopes of relief. An image of the Virgin Mary was placed outside the fort, and the Catholic ceremony of mass was performed before it. Cartier himself vowed to make a pilgrimage to a sacred place in the south of France, Roc-Amadour, if he lived long enough to return to Europe.

Since relations between the French and the Iroquois were not good, Cartier did not want them to know how sick the French party was. He feared attack if the Iroquois knew how few of his men were able-bodied. So whenever an Iroquois came near the fort, Cartier made sure that those who were healthy set up a huge racket, banging and hammering and creating the illusion of a large group at work.

The Iroquois suffered from scurvy as well. It is not known how many died from it that winter, though Cartier estimated the number as at least 50. Still, many of the Iroquois recovered quickly, and this led to relief for the French as well.

## OBSERVING THE IROQUOIS

Cartier spent much of his time during the long winter assembling a notebook of information about his surroundings. For example, he wrote that the Iroquois had few possessions beyond a store of foods, which was held more or less in common. Most of their fish and game was eaten fresh. They smoked or dried their surplus fish and game, but did not use salt as Europeans often did.

The Iroquois cultivated corn, melons, squash, and beans, and they did not have domesticated animals beyond dogs. They dressed in skins, and even in the winter wore only light clothing such as leggings and loincloths. They used pottery and had permanent, well-built residences. Widows never remarried; they marked themselves as widows with smeared grease and soot on their faces.

The Iroquois had a religious system that included their god, Cuduagny. According to their beliefs, he told them the weather and, if angry, threw dust in their eyes. The Iroquois further believed that when they died they would travel to the stars, and then sink to earth again to find hunting grounds beyond the horizon.

The Iroquois also used tobacco. According to Leacock, Cartier wrote:

> [T]hey fill their bodies full of smoke till that it cometh out of their mouths and nostrils, even as out of the funnel of a chimney. They say that it doth keep them warm and in health; they never go without some of it about them. We ourselves have tried the same smoke, and, having put it in our mouths, it seemed almost as hot as pepper.

It was Donnacona's son Domagaya who saved the explorers. Domagaya had suffered from the disease, but Cartier noticed that within days he was cured. The Frenchman did not want to reveal that most of his men were sick, so he told Domagaya that he was interested in a cure because one of his servants was ill. Domagaya explained that the answer was a tea made from the leaves of the *annedda* tree (white cedar, also known as *arborvitae*).

Although some of the Frenchmen were at first reluctant to try the cure, it proved wildly successful for them. Cartier later took samples of white cedar on his return trip—the first native North American trees transplanted to Europe. In his enthusiasm for the cure, Dawson notes that Cartier later wrote that he and his men would never have seen France again "unless God in his infinite goodness and mercy had not looked upon them in pity and given them knowledge of a remedy against all diseases, the most excellent that was ever seen or known in all the earth."

The St. Lawrence remained iced over for a particularly long time that year. Cartier was not able to leave until early May. As he prepared to sail away, the explorer realized that the midsized ship in his fleet, *La Petite Hermine*, was not seaworthy and might not survive the trip home. Furthermore, the number of able-bodied crewmembers had shrunk so there were not enough sailors to man the ship.

So the ship was abandoned in the mouth of the river where it had been moored. It stayed there, undiscovered, for more than 300 years. What are believed to be its remains were found imbedded in the river's mud in the 1840s. Some of these remains were donated to the Québec Literary and Historical Society, and some to the town of Saint-Malo.

As Cartier prepared for his departure, plots and counterplots were hatching. Donnacona had recently gone on what he said would be a short hunting trip, but he had been gone a long time. When he returned he was in the company of hostile people Cartier had never seen before. When Cartier sent a group to visit Donnacona, the Iroquois chief refused to see them. It seemed clear that Donnacona was planning something.

Part of the ongoing problem was a power struggle between Donnacona and his rival, Agona. Taignoagny asked for Cartier's help in eliminating Agona, perhaps by sending him into exile. Cartier saw a way to turn this quarrel to his advantage. Since the Frenchman felt he could no longer trust Donnacona or his sons, he decided to form an alliance with Agona, which he hoped would strengthen future French relations with the St. Lawrence Iroquois.

Cartier put his plan into action by tricking Donnacona. He pretended to agree to the plot against Agona. On May 3, the day of the feast of the Holy Cross, the Iroquois chief came to witness the raising of another cross, accompanied by his sons and several others. This was a 35-foot (10.5-meter) cross on the riverbank. It had a fleur-de-lis and a Latin inscription: *Franciscus Primus Dei Gratia Francorum Rex Regnat* ("François I, by the grace of God King of the French, is sovereign.")

Cartier invited Donnacona and the others to a feast aboard *La Grande Hermine*. The Frenchman then seized them and held them captive. When word got out, the inhabitants of Stadacona were upset, but Cartier insisted that he would bring back Donnacona in a year, along with lavish presents from the French king.

Three days later the Frenchmen sailed away. In the cargo holds of the ships were, among other goods, a dozen pieces of gold and some furs. Accompanying the Frenchmen were about 10 Iroquois, including several children, Donnacona, and his sons. By bringing Donnacona and his sons to France, Cartier served two purposes: the way would be clear for Agona to come to power, and Donnacona could tell the French king in person about the fabulous city of gold.

## Rivals

The French expedition was not the only one to have sailed from Europe for Newfoundland and the surrounding regions in search of treasure and the Northwest Passage. For several years, the English had already been serious rivals of the French in this quest.

One of the early British expeditions left England at about the same time as Cartier left Stadacona. There were two ships in this small fleet: the *Trinity* and the *Minion*, which left the port of Gravesend under the flag of the English king, Henry VIII. They carried a crew of 120, 30 of them gentlemen and the rest seamen. The person in charge was "Master How, of London, a man of goodly stature, and of great courage, and given to the study of cosmography [the study of the earth and stars]." His mission was to explore the St. Lawrence and begin a permanent colony in Newfoundland.

After landing, however, the British expedition was faced with famine. According to some sources, it was so devastating that some sailors were forced to kill and eat weaker crew-members. The remaining survivors were saved when a French fishing vessel happened to find them. The Englishmen seized the French ship and its supplies, and then returned to England with both vessels.

The owners of the French ship later brought the affair to the English court, seeking compensation and penalties. Henry VIII felt that the British seamen had been in great need, and that their actions were justified. He therefore did not punish them. However, he did pay back the owners of the ship the value of their property.

Cartier and his crew battled contrary winds on their way to the sea. The explorers slowly sailed along the southern edge of Anticosti Island, finding that it was indeed an island, and entered the gulf. As Cartier sailed across the gulf, he realized

Henry VIII, known best for having six wives, sent two ships across the Atlantic Ocean to further explore opportunities in North America. Hoping to establish a settlement in Newfoundland, crews from the *Minion* and the *Trinity* almost starved to death before capturing a French boat and returning to England.

that the Magdalen Islands, which he called the Araines, were not part of the mainland as he had thought. He also discovered the passage between Newfoundland and Cape Breton, which he had not noticed on his first voyage. Now called Cabot Strait, this is the southern entrance to the gulf from the sea.

The trip to the open sea was difficult, and the Atlantic crossing took another three weeks. Cartier did not return home until midsummer, having been gone a total of about 14 months. Cartier wrote in his journal, as quoted by Leacock, "On July 6, 1536, we reached the harbour of Saint-Malo, by the Grace of our Creator, whom we pray, making an end of our navigation, to grant us His Grace, and Paradise at the end. Amen."

## The Aftermath of the Second Voyage

Soon after he landed in Saint-Malo, Cartier made a detailed report to his king, François I. Some parts of the report were extremely discouraging. For example, the king was not happy to hear about the bleakness of the Canadian winter, the hostility of the Iroquois, and the inability of the explorers to find the kingdom of gold.

On the other hand, the explorer's second voyage had been overall much more successful than his first. Cartier had found a new access route to the gulf. He discovered a river that led deep into the unexplored continent. He told the king that this river measured at least 800 leagues. (A league was the distance a typical man could walk in one hour. It was equal to about 3.5 miles or 5.5 km.) Cartier told the king that he hoped the river led to Asia.

Another success of this trip was that Cartier saw the many natural resources of that river's valley. He made more accurate maps of the regions he saw than had previously existed. And he found at least some gold, though not the great riches for which he had hoped.

Finally, Cartier had made connections with the inhabitants of the new land (though not all of his actions toward them were honorable). He wrote detailed information about them, and he came back with a chieftain who boasted of having visited a fabulously wealthy country. The grateful king presented Cartier with his primary ship, *La Grande Hermine,* as a reward for his successes.

François was even more greatly encouraged when he listened to the stories Donnacona told through an interpreter. Donnacona agreed with Cartier's belief that the St. Lawrence River did indeed stretch to Asia. The Iroquois chief also told many other wonderful stories to the king and other French authorities, including monk and historian André Thevet, who specialized in interrogating travelers. Donnacona spoke of large numbers of fur-bearing animals in Canada's woods and waters. He praised its abundant salmon, the richness of its soil, and the value of its timber.

He also insisted that he had visited the fabulous Saguenay, where, he said, the land was rich with mines of gold and silver. He claimed that the land there also had an abundance of cloves, nutmeg, and pepper, valuable and rare spices that Europeans craved. And he mentioned many other marvels, such as a race of men, each with one leg, and men who flew with wings on their arms like bats.

Some of the members of the king's court questioned these stories. They wondered if much of his information was simply storytelling to please and perhaps fool the French. They also wondered if perhaps Donnacona was simply spinning tales to ensure another expedition—one that would return him home.

François was very enthusiastic and chose to believe the Iroquois chief. Historian Eccles notes that this "information, learned from the Indians and embroidered by the greedy imaginations of [the] Europeans, [was] that gold, silver, spices, and a people with a very advanced civilization were to be found in the interior." François was therefore eager to sponsor another expedition. Finding the Northwest Passage, however, was not as high a priority as it once was. Instead, two things particularly raised the king's interest: finding the kingdom of gold and creating a permanent colony for France.

# The Third Voyage Begins

It was not possible for France to mount another expedition to the New World immediately. Several things contributed to this. Chief among them was a drawn-out and costly war with François's sworn enemy, Charles V, the ruler of Spain. The war was draining France's resources, and so François could not seriously plan new expeditions to the New World for some time. It was not until the war with Spain temporarily ended in June 1538 that the New World once again became a concern for the king of France.

When François did turn his attention that way, he realized that Charles was using the vast fortunes being earned by Spain's New World colonies to finance his military. This convinced François that exploration was worthwhile. He reasoned that he might prevail on the battlefield if France could similarly earn money from its colonies. (In fact, the two monarchs did go to war again later.)

Upon his return to France, Cartier presented reports of his findings and his captive, Chief Donnacona, to François I, the king of France. While the monarch was enthusiastic and intrigued at what France could potentially gain from further exploration of the New World, he could not finance another expedition for some time due to war with Spain's Charles V. Only later, when the two royals agreed to a truce with the Treaty of Nice in 1538 *(depicted above)*, did François I provide funds for Cartier's third voyage.

## The Years in Between

It is not known for certain what Cartier did during the years before François ordered another voyage. The only official record of his activities came in May 1537, when the king formally made his gift to Cartier of his flagship, *La Grande Hermine*. Trudel writes of this period, "Cartier seems to have been reduced to inactivity."

There is some evidence that Cartier wrote a memoir in 1538, but the authenticity of this book has never been proven. There is also some evidence that he became a pirate, using *La Grande Hermine* to loot Spanish and Portuguese ships. (This was not an uncommon practice for European explorers when they were between expeditions.) And there is some evidence that Cartier gave aid to an Irishman named Gerald Fitzgerald who was leading a rebellion against England.

There is also very little detail known about what happened during these years to the Iroquois whom Cartier brought to France. It is known that in March 1539 three of them were baptized and became Christians. It is not known if Donnacona was one of the three, although Thevet, the monk, wrote that this was so. What is certain is that Donnacona and all but one of the Iroquois who had been held captive died before they could return home. The exception was a little girl.

In October 1540, Cartier finally received a formal commission concerning a third voyage. Money was set aside to equip eight ships and prepare hundreds of people for the trip. The voyage's main goal was to create a permanent settlement. This colony would then establish a trading company. According to the formal commission, the land where the colony was to be built was still considered a portion of Asia. Another goal was to find the fabled kingdom of Saguenay.

In his royal decrees concerning Cartier's third voyage, King François made clear the details of the mission, including the appointment of Roberval as the official head of the expedition. François also explained that France's prisons would be searched for "volunteer" colonists. The king announced:

> Whereas we have undertaken this voyage for the honor
> of God our Creator, desiring with all our heart to do

that which shall be agreeable to Him, it is our will to perform a compassionate and meritorious work towards criminals and malefactors, to the end that they may acknowledge the Creator, return thanks to Him, and mend their lives. Therefore we have resolved to cause to be delivered to our aforesaid lieutenant [Roberval], such and so many of the aforesaid criminals and malefactors detained in our prisons as may seem to him useful and necessary to be carried to the aforesaid countries.

As the preparations for the voyage began, the activities around Saint-Malo aroused the curiosity and suspicions of François's old enemy, Charles of Spain. The Spanish king sent a number of spies to the French port. They had orders to report back to him about the planned expedition.

One big reason why Charles was worried about a French voyage was simply financial. Spanish colonies were already being established in the Caribbean, South America, and in what is today Mexico and the southern United States. Thanks to the abundance of such treasures as gold and silver, these colonies were fabulously profitable. Charles was worried that the French might move south from Canada and creep in on the land already claimed for Spain—or that François might find similar riches in Canada, and would therefore be in a strong position to renew his war against Spain.

Others in Spain were not worried about the French efforts. They scoffed that the only valuable goods the French would find were fish. The Cardinal of Seville commented, according to historian Dawson, "The motives of the French are that they suppose these lands to be rich in gold and silver. In my opinion they are wrong, because the whole coast [of North America] as far as Florida contains no other wealth than that dependent on fisheries."

## Enter Roberval

It was logical to think that Cartier would be the leader of this new expedition, as he had been earlier. In January 1541, however, the situation changed dramatically. At that time, François placed Jean-François de La Rocque de Roberval at the head of the project.

Roberval, as he was called, was a member of the king's court, a military officer, a longtime friend of François, and a nobleman. What he was *not* was an explorer or a navigator. Although he was a professional military man, Roberval had no special experience at sea or in new lands.

As the head of this great adventure, Roberval received a suitably grand title: "Lord of Norumbega, viceroy and lieutenant-general of Canada, Hochelaga, Saguenay, Newfoundland, Belle Isle, Carpunt, Labrador, the Great Bay, and Bacalaos." Norumbega was a name then used for the area that made up what is now the U.S. state of Maine and the Canadian provinces of New Brunswick and Nova Scotia. Bacalaos was another name for Newfoundland, and Carpunt is a harbor near Belle Isle.

One important reason for the appointment of Roberval was to make the powerful Catholic Church see the importance of the new colony. By seeking to establish a new colony in North America, France was challenging an already-established right of the Catholic Pope to divide up the land of the New World as he saw fit.

François maintained that only the physical occupation of a land was required to claim it, not the Pope's authority. But he needed a strong and aristocratic man at the head of his new colony to make it legitimate. Even though Roberval was a Protestant, not a Catholic, he was chosen to fill the position. It seems a common sailor such as Cartier could not be entrusted with this role.

For the third voyage, King François I passed over Cartier and appointed Jean-François de La Rocque de Roberval *(above)* as lieutenant-general of his Canadian territories. Because the Roman Catholic Church had taken responsibility for allotting New World territories to European countries, the French king decided to circumvent their authority by drafting Roberval, a Protestant, to establish a settlement in North America.

François named Cartier "Captain and Pilot of the King." This made Cartier the chief mariner of the expedition, commanding a fleet of five ships (out of eight total). These were *La Grande Hermine* and *L'Émérillon* from the second expedition, as well as the *Saint-Breux,* the *Saint-Georges*, and a fifth vessel whose name has been lost to historians.

But Cartier's position was a lower rank than the one that Roberval held. It meant that Cartier now had to follow Roberval's orders. Roberval had ultimate authority over all of the expedition's ships—Cartier's as well as his own—and over the people on board. He also had the power to appoint or remove new captains and pilots, to build forts in the new colony, and even to grant portions of land to loyal followers.

There is no record of Cartier's feelings on the matter, but this secondary arrangement was undoubtedly insulting to the veteran navigator. Historian Dawson comments, "The experienced and successful sailor who had conducted two expeditions with success was rudely deposed and put under the command of a courtier, a landsman, a soldier, a person of no experience, not even of special note in the history of the time."

## Preparing for the Voyage

No matter his feelings on the subject, Cartier's preparations for the voyage moved swiftly. He equipped his ships and assembled enough food to last for two years. Among this store of food was a large group of livestock: 20 cows, 4 bulls, 100 sheep, 100 goats, 10 hogs, and 20 horses.

He also found his crew and his passengers, the people who were to become members of the new colony. Trudel notes that these people were to be, in the words of the royal commission, "of willing disposition and of all professions, arts and industries." The passengers included nobles, doctors, priests, carpenters, ironworkers, farmers, barbers, pharmacists, craftsmen, and tailors—every trade that was seen as being necessary to establish a new city. According to archaeologist Jean Provencher, "They dreamed of remaking French society [in Canada]."

Many noblemen were also eager to come along on the expedition, lured by the promise of riches. They expected to receive a third of the profits from the land they would be given in the New World, with the rest of the profits divided between Roberval and the king.

The plan for finding the rest of the colony's future population was to look in the world of sailors and soldiers, plus find a few women. Cartier, however, had difficulty finding enough people to fill the ranks. Many potential volunteers were likely scared away from the mission by stories they heard about the difficulty of life in the New World. There were other potential dangers and sorrows as well, as François himself pointed out. He said that many people were fearful of the voyage, Trudel notes, "because of the far distance of these lands and the dread of shipwrecks and maritime and other hazards, [and being unwilling] to leave their possessions, relatives and friends."

As a result, Cartier and Roberval had to add to their roster of volunteers with about 50 men recruited from the prisons of France. Many of these were given the promise of having their death sentences taken away, and of the possibility of returning to France, if they agreed to go to the new colony. They were responsible for paying their own way on the sea voyage, and earning their keep in Canada for two years. They would then be eligible to return with full pardons.

By May 1541, Cartier's five ships were ready to leave Saint-Malo. Roberval and his three ships, however, were not. The nobleman had not yet received all of the artillery and supplies he had ordered from the nearby regions of Champagne and Normandy, and he was forced to wait.

Cartier was therefore given special permission by the king to leave ahead of Roberval. François gave Cartier specific authority to represent France in Roberval's absence. Among the officers on Cartier's ships were two of his brothers-in-law—Guyon des Granches, the viscount of Beaupré, and a pilot, Macé Jalobert. One of Cartier's nephews, Étienne Noël, was also on board. Notable among the rest of the crew was a shipmaster, Thomas Fromont, who served as Cartier's assistant on *La Grande Hermine*.

Cartier, the crew, and the passengers assembled in the cathedral of Saint-Malo to receive the church's blessings, as they had in the past. Then Cartier's five ships left the port on May 23, bound for the New World. The exact number of people aboard is uncertain, but one Spanish spy put the total at 1,500.

## Returning to Stadacona

It was a difficult crossing. Bad winds and storms slowed the passage of the ships, and it took about three months. Partway across the ocean they ran out of fresh water. The crew had to tap the ship's store of cider casks in order to give the goats and cattle enough liquid to drink.

After finally making landfall, the group anchored at Belle Isle. They repaired and refitted the ships while they waited for Roberval. But he did not arrive, so Cartier's ships headed once again to Stadacona. They reached the Iroquois village late in August. Cartier found a situation there that was partly to his advantage. As the Frenchman had hoped, Agona had taken Donnacona's place. Furthermore, the new chief still seemed friendly toward the explorers.

The people of Stadacona were very upset when they learned that Donnacona was not on board the French ships. Cartier had to tell them that Donnacona had died in France. This was the truth. But Cartier also told the group a lie. He stated that the other chiefs were still living in luxury in France, and that they had no intention of returning. In fact, only the one little girl had survived. The reasons for the deaths are not certain, but

On Cartier's third voyage, he revisited the site of Stadacona and then continued along the St. Lawrence River until he reached the Rivière Cap-Rouge (Cap Rouge River). A tributary of the St. Lawrence, the site of the Cap Rouge River *(above)* became Charlesbourg-Royal, the first French settlement in North America.

it has been speculated that they died through a combination of strange food and environment.

The residents of Stadacona were furious that Cartier had taken their chiefs, and they were mistrustful of his intentions. Despite Agona's seeming friendliness, Cartier decided not to remain in the village. Instead, he sailed a few miles upriver. He chose to stop where the Rivière Cap-Rouge (Cap Rouge River) empties into the St. Lawrence. It was here that he built a settlement, which he called Charlesbourg-Royal. It was the first permanent French settlement in North America. On this site today is the town of Cap-Rouge, a suburb of Quebec City.

At first, this site seemed to be a favorable spot. For one thing, there was plenty of white cedar around that the settlers could use against the threat of scurvy. Also, there were other abundant natural resources, including timber, fertile land, and wild grapes.

Furthermore, soon after landing the crew found many stones in the surrounding land. They believed that these were precious treasures. Cartier noted that they were "slate, stone with mineral veins looking like gold and silver, and stones like diamonds, the most fair-polished and excellent cut that it is possible for a man to see. When the sun shineth upon them they glisten as if it were sparkles of fire," writes Dawson.

A lot of work was necessary to create the settlement. Once Cartier's crew and passengers were ashore, they had to build shelters, plow land for crops, and start gardens. They had to unload and pen the cattle and other livestock that had survived the three months of rough seas across the Atlantic. And, because they were not sure how relations with the Iroquois would be, they had to build a fortified embankment around their settlement. For added protection, Cartier ordered that another fort be built. Situated on the cliff overlooking Charlesbourg-Royal, it provided a good lookout over the river and the land around. The new colony was now ready to survive a winter.

# The Third Voyage Ends

As the colonists were creating their settlement, Cartier took care of other tasks. He was eager to report back to France that his group was so far successful, and also that Roberval had not yet arrived. On September 2, the pilot sent two ships (the *Saint-Georges* and the *Saint-Brieux*) back across the Atlantic, under the command of Jalobert and Noël. They arrived in Saint-Malo in mid-October.

Meanwhile, Cartier himself left Charlesbourg-Royal in the opposite direction on September 7. His mission was to take two longboats farther up the river, to look again at the rapids that had blocked his path to Saguenay on the earlier trip. He hoped that by exploring the region more thoroughly he could find an opening that would let him pass in the spring. Cartier's brother-in-law, the viscount of Beaupré, remained behind in Charlesbourg-Royal and was put in charge of the settlement.

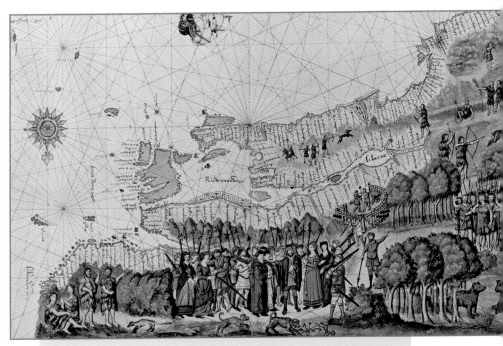

After leaving the unprepared Roberval behind in France, Cartier established Charlesbourg-Royal, a few miles upstream from Stadacona. Due to the time of their arrival, Cartier immediately instructed his crew and the colonists to begin unloading the ships *(above)*, building forts, and planting gardens to prepare for the upcoming winter.

Along the way Cartier stopped at the small village of Hochelay, where he had spent time on his previous voyage, and left two of his young crew members there. He gave them instructions that they should learn the language, so that they could become interpreters. They were the first two Europeans to become pupils of the Iroquois.

On September 11, Cartier reached the rapids that had blocked his way earlier, upriver from Hochelaga. Despite his best effort, however, he was unable to get past them. Even after putting extra rowers in one of the boats for power, they could not navigate the swift rapids and enormous rocks.

A group of North American Indians whom Cartier met near the rapids told him that there were still more rapids upstream. They used sticks laid on the ground to explain their meaning, since there were no interpreters, so it remained unclear if this is what they meant. In any case, since he could not get past the first rapids, Cartier had no choice but to return to Charlesbourg-Royal.

## Another Hard Winter

On his return downriver, he stopped again at Hochelay, but found that it was nearly abandoned and the boys he had left there were gone. Their fate is unknown. When Cartier got back to Charlesbourg-Royal, it was clear that while he was gone relations with the Iroquois had seriously worsened even further. Even those Iroquois whom Cartier had previously considered allies were now openly distrustful of him.

The reasons for this are not entirely clear. One theory takes note of the fact that many of the new colonists were criminals taken from the prisons of France. It is possible that these criminals may have stolen from the Iroquois or committed other crimes. Also, there was still lingering anger over Cartier's failure to bring Donnacona back to Stadacona. Furthermore, there was now no doubt that the French explorers intended to make a permanent settlement in the St. Lawrence Valley, and the Iroquois were understandably angry.

Despite what seemed like growing tension between the two groups, Cartier and the rest of the French expedition began to prepare for spending a long and difficult winter in Charlesbourg-Royal. As quoted in Leacock, Cartier's narrative of this period (in which he refers to himself in the third person) ends with an explicit statement that the fort needed to be made ready in case of attack:

> And when we were arrived at our fort, we understood by
> our people that the savages of the country came not any

more about our fort, as they were accustomed to bring us fish, and that they were in a wonderful doubt and fear of us. Wherefore our captain, having been advised by some of our men which had been at Stadacona to visit them that there was a wonderful number of the country people [Iroquois] assembled together, caused all things in our fortress to be set in good order.

Roberval never arrived at Charlesbourg-Royal. Cartier, of course, had no idea what had happened to him and his party. Meanwhile, winter came early that year, and soon Cartier's encampment—it appears that there were about 400 people there at this point—was snowed in and the river iced over.

There are few written details about Charlesbourg-Royal during this winter, because Cartier's journal covering this period ends abruptly. It is a safe assumption that the winter was a grim one. The settlement was probably at times nearly buried in snowdrifts. Scurvy likely continued to be a problem, though it would have been solved with white cedar tea. In any case, the death toll was dramatically lower compared with the previous winter the French had spent in Canada.

More serious than before, however, were the poor relations with the increasingly angry Iroquois. There is some evidence that the Iroquois practically kept the French prisoners in their fort by laying siege to it. They also made periodic attacks on the settlement, killing an estimated 35 people. It is not known how many Iroquois were killed in return, or how many died of other causes.

By the time the ice finally broke in the river the following spring, the colony's supplies were nearly gone. Cartier felt that he did not have enough able-bodied men either to protect his base at Charlesbourg-Royal or to go in search of the long-sought kingdom of Saguenay. He decided, therefore, to leave for home while he was still able to do so. The colony broke down camp in June 1542 and set sail down the river.

## Reunion

When he reached the harbor that is now called St. John's, on Newfoundland, Cartier had a surprise waiting for him. In the harbor were three ships, with Roberval in charge and about 200 colonists, noblemen, and sailors aboard. Also in the harbor were about 20 French fishing vessels that had already been in the area.

When Cartier and Roberval were reunited, Roberval reported that he had not left France until April 16, 1542, and that he had reached St. John's on June 8. He and his ships had been in the harbor for only a few days when Cartier arrived. Roberval's supplies had been so late in arriving, he reported, that he had been forced to spend the winter of 1541 to 1542 on the French coast. While he waited, the nobleman had pirated various ships in the English Channel. This seems to be the kind of work that Roberval preferred over colonization, and he had been happy to winter over in France. He was in no hurry to reach the harsh New World. Dawson comments, "This work [of pirating] was more congenial to his nature than colonisation."

For his part, Cartier reported that he had left Charlesbourg-Royal because supplies were running desperately low, and because the Iroquois were becoming increasingly hostile. Also, though the land was relatively fertile, it was not good enough to sustain the kind of farming he had envisioned. Furthermore, although he was transporting a small quantity of what he believed were diamonds and gold, Cartier had failed to find the legendary city of gold.

Cartier strongly advised Roberval to turn around and not to attempt going farther up the river. The viceroy, however, thought that Cartier was simply being selfish. He suspected that Cartier wanted to receive all the honor of his discoveries himself, as well as the distinction of having founded the first French colony. Roberval further accused Cartier of abandoning his post too soon. Asserting his superior rank, Roberval ordered Cartier, along with all his crew and passengers, to return with him to the settlement. He was convinced that their combined forces would be enough to overcome the North American Indians.

Cartier thought Roberval was a careless and unskilled leader, and so he disobeyed him. Under the cover of a cloudy and moonless night, the pilot quietly led his vessels from the harbor and set sail for Saint-Malo. In addition to his crew of sailors, Cartier took with him a military detachment and those colonists who wanted to return to France. He was determined not to spend another winter in Canada—especially not under Roberval. According to Dawson, "Cartier and his companions had suffered enough from Roberval, and would not risk a winter in Canada under his inexperienced command."

By sneaking out, Cartier deprived his rival Roberval of vital information about survival in the New World, as well as denying him crucial extra manpower. Cartier also had what he thought was treasure: several barrels of what he believed to be gold, precious stones, and silver.

## Another Hard Winter

Cartier and his ships arrived back in Saint-Malo in September 1542. His return brought to a conclusion what proved to be his last voyage. It may have been his last because François was angry with him for disobeying Roberval and returning to France. No proof, however, has ever been found that the king officially scolded or punished Cartier. In any case, for whatever reason, the explorer never again received a royal commission or mounted a major voyage.

Meanwhile, even after Cartier's secret departure, Roberval chose to carry on westward. He and his captains had copies of the maps that Cartier had made of the river. These were well made and generally accurate, so Roberval was able to use them to pass without incident through the Strait of Belle Isle and into the St. Lawrence.

Roberval and his group found the forts that had been constructed and abandoned by Cartier at Charlesbourg-Royal. They decided to use these to establish their own settlement, rather than building from scratch. Roberval called this revived settlement France-Roy. He and his men turned it into a fortified encampment that included lookout towers, grain mills, baking ovens, barracks for the soldiers, and sleeping quarters for the rest of the group.

But the new colony lasted less than a year. Another severe winter, an outbreak of scurvy, and periodic attacks by the Iroquois took a heavy toll. At least 50 colonists died. Furthermore, Roberval and his group lost a ship and 8 more men in June, when he led them on a failed mission in search of the kingdom of gold.

Those who survived that winter had to deal not only with horrific weather and hostile natives, but also with the violent and arrogant Roberval himself. Anyone who complained about the scanty, rat-infested, often moldy rations they were given was whipped, beaten, or imprisoned. Some who dared to defy Roberval were hanged or shot. Thevet, the French monk who wrote extensively about the North American expeditions, commented:

> Forced to unceasing labour and chafed by arbitrary rules, some of the soldiers fell under Roberval's displeasure, and six of them, formerly his favourites, were hanged in one day. Others were banished to an island and there kept in fetters [chains]; while for various offences several, both men and women, were shot. Even the Indians were moved to pity and wept at the sight of their woes.

In contrast, there has never been any evidence that Cartier displayed similar cruelty toward his men on any of his voyages.

Indeed, he seems to have been considerably more humane than many European explorers in similar positions during those years. As a result, he generally inspired loyalty among his crew. Dawson comments, "Cartier conducted three expeditions, and his men gave him the willing obedience which only a competent master can obtain."

Roberval proved to be an incompetent and arrogant leader, characteristics that pushed Cartier to secretly set sail for France with his crew and a few colonists who wished to return to Europe. Roberval's failure to maintain his French settlement soon forced the nobleman to leave Canada as well. It would be another 60 years until Samuel de Champlain successfully established Quebec City *(above)*, the first successful French colony in Canada.

In the summer of 1543, a relief expedition arrived from France to see how Roberval and his group were doing. Some sources say that Cartier led the rescue expedition, although this seems unlikely. In any case, Roberval chose to leave France-Roy and return with his colonists to France. He, and they, had concluded that Canada was too harsh a land to support a permanent settlement.

By this time, François was once again at war with his old enemy, Charles of Spain. Roberval went back into active military service to serve the king and died in 1561. The exact circumstances of his death are murky. Leacock writes, "Certain chroniclers have said that he made another voyage to the New World and perished at sea. Others have it that he was assassinated in Paris near the Church of the Holy Innocents. But nothing is known."

Roberval's failed settlement of France-Roy was the last permanent French settlement in North America for more than 60 years. Not until 1608, when Samuel Champlain founded a trading station in what is now Quebec City, would the French have a major presence there.

## A Disappointment

All in all, Canada had proved to be a disappointment. The land was reasonably fertile, but it grew more or less the same crops as could be grown in Europe. The winters were terribly harsh. No valuable spices and no passage to Asia had been found.

Furthermore, the supposed treasures Cartier brought back were a disappointment. What the explorer thought was gold proved to be nothing more than iron pyrites, sometimes called "fool's gold." The diamonds, meanwhile, were only quartz crystals. In time, this experience gave rise to a French expression: *Faux comme les diamants du Canada*, which means "As false as Canadian diamonds."

So there was little reason for the French to explore the region anymore, much less to settle permanently. Eccles notes, "Great hopes had been riding on the [Cartier/Roberval] enterprise. They had now been shattered. The disappointment was terrible. Suddenly, Canada had become a savage country, offering nothing of value, leading nowhere, and uninhabitable for Europeans half the year. French interest in the region vanished."

The same held true for other Europeans. As far as is known, no other explorers from a European nation traveled up the St. Lawrence for another 40 years. In fact, for decades there was barely even any exploration anywhere in the region, by the French or any other nation.

On the other hand, the fishing fleets along the eastern coast continued to flourish and grow. By the end of the sixteenth century, an estimated 500 European ships annually fished in what are now Canadian waters. Furthermore, Basque fishermen from Spain established a whale station on the St. Lawrence at the mouth of the Saguenay River.

Cartier's role in the exploration of the St. Lawrence had ended, but the European presence in North America had not. As for the explorer himself, he settled into a comfortable life on shore.

# Cartier's Final Years

THERE WERE MANY LOOSE ENDS TO BE TIED UP IN THE WAKE of the failed colonial expedition. First, there was the matter of money spent. Cartier apparently never gained great wealth of any kind from his pioneering adventures. In fact, on his final voyage he had been forced to use a good deal of his own money.

In the spring of 1544, well after Roberval had returned to France, a special trial was assembled so that the financial accounts of Roberval and Cartier could be settled. During the course of this trial, Cartier was able to prove that he had budgeted well and honorably, without waste. As a result, François paid him about 9,000 *livres*. The livre was the currency of France at the time, and the sum paid to Cartier was huge. For comparison, 200 livres was a comfortable year's salary for a professional. Later, in 1588, a few merchants in Saint-Malo claimed that they never received money that Cartier owed them, but this was never proven.

# In Church and Court

Once the trial ended, Cartier apparently spent most of his time on business, which included managing Limoilou, his small estate outside Saint-Malo. Only a few details about his life during this time are known. For example, it is recorded in city documents that he served as a witness at court on several occasions.

Cartier was fluent in Portuguese, and so he was sometimes called on to be an interpreter in various places, including the courts. Historian Samuel Edward Dawson notes one such instance: "[O]n one occasion [Cartier] was called upon to testify to the sufficiency of an interpreter in a trial at Saint-Malo for the adjudication [judging] of a Portuguese prize taken by some Breton privateers [pirates]."

The mariner was also asked to be a godfather on many occasions. Records indicate he was present at more than 70 baptisms in his lifetime. A note in the city registry that was connected with baptisms associates him with the town's "other hearty drinkers" (*et aultres bons biberons*, in the French spelling of the day). Baptisms were occasions for great feasting and drinking, so this fits in with the custom of the times.

Cartier is repeatedly referred to in such records as *un noble homme*, or "a noble man," although he was not an aristocrat by birth. This indicates that, late in his life, the people of Saint-Malo considered him to be a respected member of the well-established *bourgeoisie*, the upper-middle classes.

Little more is known about Cartier's life, however, in the years after his great voyages. His wife, Katherine (also spelled Catherine) des Granches, died in April 1575. They had no children, or at least none who survived into adulthood. Two of his nephews succeeded him as master pilots of Saint-Malo.

Jacques Cartier died on September 1, 1557. He was 66 years old.

# Accounts of Cartier's Voyages

Accounts of all three of Cartier's voyages were published at various times and in various languages. For example, an account of the first expedition was published some years after the fact: in Italian in 1565; in English in 1580; and in French in 1598.

An account of the second voyage was published in French as early as 1545. Its title is *Bref récit et succincte narration de la navigation faite en MDXXXV et MDXXXVI* ("Short account and succinct narration of the voyage made in 1535 and 1536"). The book was published anonymously, and Cartier is mentioned only once by name. Instead, it refers to the voyage's leader in the third person, as "our captain" or "the captain."

This indirect reference, plus its flowery language, has led some historians to question whether Cartier—by all accounts a plainspoken mariner—actually wrote the account himself. Others have suggested that Cartier wrote it with the Franciscan monk André Thevet, the same person who had interviewed Donnacona in earlier years. Another theory is that Thevet or another writer composed it using Cartier's notebooks and logbooks. And some sources suggest that the author was actually Jehan Poullet, a Breton sailor who was with Cartier on this second voyage.

An account of the third voyage, meanwhile, today exists only as an incomplete version in English that was compiled in 1600.

Cartier's travels may also have supplied inspiration for fiction. According to legend, the writer François Rabelais used Cartier's adventures for the voyages described in his famous satirical novel *Pantagruel*. The novel tells about the fantastical journeys of a father-and-son set of giants. This theory, however, has never been proven.

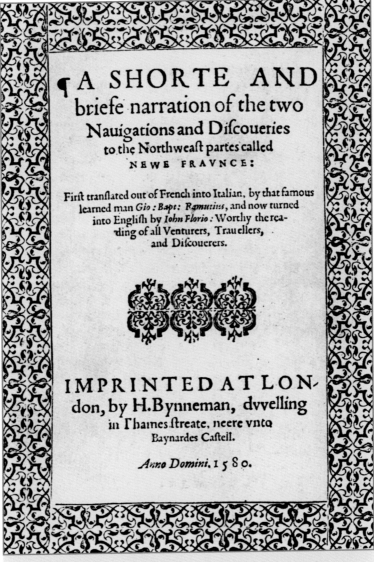

¶ A SHORTE AND
briefe narration of the two
Nauigations and Discoueries
to the Northweast partes called
NEWE FRAVNCE:

First translated out of French into Italian, by that famous
learned man *Gio : Bapt : Ramutius*, and now turned
into English by *Iohn Florio :* Worthy the reading of all Venturers, Trauellers,
and Discouerers.

IMPRINTED AT LON-
don, by H.Bynneman, dvvelling
in Thames streate, neere vnto
Baynardes Castell.

*Anno Domini.* 1 5 8 0.

Cartier's third voyage to the New World was his last and, after tying up loose ends with King François I, he continued to live out the rest of his life in Saint-Malo. As a respected, popular member of the local community, he was frequently asked to serve as a godfather, as well as a translator. Three books about his experiences were published in several languages. Above, the title page of the 1580 edition of one of Cartier's books.

## THE REALITY OF CANADA

The distinguished Canadian writer Stephen Leacock wrote a classic book about Cartier. In this excerpt, he reflects on the explorer's legacy and lasting fame:

> There is no need to enlarge upon the greatness of Cartier's achievements. It was only the beginning of a far-reaching work, the completion of which fell into other hands. But it is Cartier's proud place in history to bear the title of discoverer of a country whose annals were later to be illumined by [future explorers]. . . .
>
> Jacques Cartier, as much as perhaps any man of his time, embodied in himself what was highest in the spirit of his age. . . . He came to these coasts to find a pathway to the empire of the East. He found instead a country vast and beautiful beyond his dreams. . . . Asia was forgotten before the reality of Canada.

A related problem to the authenticity of Cartier's books is the question of portraits of the explorer. Many drawings and paintings of Cartier exist, including several sketches that appeared on various maps of the time. However, none of these portraits has been proven beyond a doubt to be authentic.

## A Discovery and a Legacy

For centuries, it was widely believed that no physical traces of Cartier's explorations still existed, apart from maps and the remains of his abandoned ship, discovered in the 1840s. But in 2005 a group of Canadian archaeologists led by Yves Chrétien made a remarkable discovery: the remains of Cartier's failed colony of Charlesbourg-Royal, the first French settlement in Canada.

Found in a hill in Cap Rouge, about 6.2 miles (10 km) from the center of Quebec City, it is considered the most important Canadian archaeological find since the 1960 discovery of a Viking village dating from A.D.1000 in northern Newfoundland. Historian Jean Provencher comments, "It is a unique discovery. We have discovered what, with Anse aux Meadows in Newfoundland [the Viking settlement], is the oldest European settlement north of Mexico."

The scientists found two main pieces of evidence that led to their conclusion. The first consisted of some remnants of burned wooden foundations that dated to the mid-sixteenth century. (Roberval had ordered the fort burned when he deserted it, to prevent it from falling into the hands of the Spanish or the Iroquois.) When they were discovered, the foundations were encrusted in clay that had baked in the fire, thus preserving the wood.

The other important artifact was a piece of a blue decorative plate. The archaeologists were able to tell that it had been manufactured in Faenza, Italy, between 1540 and 1550. According to the archaeologists, it could only have belonged to a member of the French aristocracy, probably Roberval. Also uncovered was a shard of Iroquois pottery from about the same period, along with more than 150 objects such as ceramics, pottery, nails, a ring, glass beads, vessels, and an ax.

This discovery rekindled interest in an explorer who was already a hero in Canada. Cartier is still remembered today because of the important role he holds in the history of North American exploration. It is true that he did not succeed in tracing the entire length of the St. Lawrence—that was left to later voyagers. He did, however, make crucial contributions.

He was the first European to explore beyond the shores of Newfoundland, which previously had only been visited by fishermen and skirted by explorers. Cartier thus began the great adventure of penetrating to the heartland of North America. Later explorers, notably Samuel de Champlain, extended Cartier's discoveries as he had extended those of earlier voyagers. Reaching the Great Lakes and beyond, these later French explorers in time helped create New France, a portion of North America that was many times larger than France itself.

Cartier was also the first to survey and map the coasts of the Gulf of St. Lawrence. He was the first to describe in writing the life, religion, and customs of the North American Indians of the northeastern part of the continent. This information proved vital to later explorers and settlers.

Furthermore, he was the first European to discover the St. Lawrence River, one of the great rivers of the world and the axis of the future French empire in North America. Cartier's voyages thus marked the beginning of an important part of history: France's occupation of a significant part of the continent. This occupation is still felt today, particularly in the importance of the French language and culture in eastern Canada.

Some historians have questioned Cartier's abilities as an explorer. For one thing, he failed to find a way to explore the St. Lawrence beyond the obstacle today called the Lachine Rapids. This is a minority opinion. Overall, there is little argument that Cartier was an excellent sailor and navigator. He spearheaded three voyages into dangerous, largely unknown waters without losing a single ship. (The ship left behind for the return portion of the second voyage, abandoned for lack of sufficient crew, was deliberately given up, not lost.) Also, virtually the only crewmen he lost were due to scurvy outbreaks. Furthermore, he explored roughly 50 previously undiscovered harbors with no serious accidents.

As a result of these accomplishments, Cartier is generally considered one of the period's most thorough and reliable explorers. Historians disagree somewhat, however, on the question of whether Cartier is actually the first European to

JACQUES CARTIER
1534
+
BUSTE GRACIEUSEMENT
OFFERT
PAR
LA
FRANCE
LE
1ᴱᴿ SEPTEMBRE
1934
POUR COMMEMORER LE
IVᴱ
CENTENAIRE
DE
LA NAISSANCE
DU
CANADA

Cartier's accomplishments and legacy are remembered in both Canada and France. His discovery of the St. Lawrence River was one of the major events that would encourage the European powers to establish settlements and colonize North America. Today, several monuments and structures are dedicated to the French explorer, including this bust in Saint-Malo.

"discover Canada." The answer is no, if "Canada" refers to the entire nation as it is today. In fact, he explored only a tiny part of that vast nation.

If the term is taken to mean the Canada of Cartier's own time, the answer is clearly yes. "Canada" in the sixteenth century meant only the region that extended roughly from Stadacona (where Quebec City stands today) to Hochelaga (the site of present-day Montreal).

Furthermore, Cartier was the first to use that name for the land extending inland from the sea, and the first to call the natives of that region *Canadiens* ("Canadians"). It is true that the name "Canada" was mistakenly used, since it was the Iroquois word for "village" and Cartier thought they were referring to the land in general. Nonetheless, the word came to mean the region around the colony that France tried to establish, and eventually included all of the land in the present-day nation.

## Honors After Death

Cartier's accomplishments are honored today, hundreds of years after his death, in a number of ways. For example, a major street in the old part of Montreal is called Place Jacques-Cartier. His name is also used to designate a river, a bridge, a park, an island, and many other features in Canada.

Of course, Cartier is also remembered in the city of his birth, which today is one of the most popular tourist cities in Brittany. A statue of the explorer prominently stands in the Old City, the original walled portion of Saint-Malo. A popular hotel named in his honor is also in the ancient part of the city. And Cartier's estate, Limoilou, is now a museum devoted to him.

In 2005, the *Literary Review of Canada* gave an important honor to the *Brif récit*, the volume documenting Cartier's second voyage. The journal named it the most important book in Canadian history. Thanks to such recent honors, it is unlikely that the name of Jacques Cartier will disappear from the history books. He remains one of the greatest explorers of one of history's greatest and most exciting eras of exploration.

# CHRONOLOGY

| 1491 | Cartier is born in Saint-Malo, Brittany (later part of France). |
| 1519 or 1520 | Cartier marries Marie Katherine des Granches, the daughter of a prominent family. |
| 1534 | APRIL  Cartier leaves on his first voyage of discovery to North America. |
| | JUNE  Cartier has his first encounter with North American Indians, a group of Beothuk seal hunters. |

## TIMELINE

APRIL  Cartier leaves on his first voyage of discovery to North America

JULY  Cartier meets Donnacona and other members of the St. Lawrence Iroquois tribe and takes Donnacona's two sons with him

AUGUST  On his second voyage, Cartier uses the name "Canada" in his logbook; names a bay "St. Laurent," the name later given to the entire system of waterways

**1491**

**1535**

**1534**

Cartier is born in Saint-Malo, Brittany (later part of France)

1535–1536
Cartier and his party winter near Stadacona; he returns to France with Donnacona and his sons

JULY    Cartier meets members of the Micmac tribe on a fishing expedition; Cartier meets Donnacona and other members of the St. Lawrence Iroquois tribe and takes Donnacona's two sons with him.

AUGUST    Cartier's ships start the return journey to France and arrive in September.

**1535**    MAY    Cartier leaves on his second voyage and arrives in July.

AUGUST    Cartier uses the name "Canada" in his logbook, the first-known written mention of that name; Cartier names a bay "St. Laurent," the name later given to the entire system of waterways.

SEPTEMBER    Cartier arrives in Stadacona, the home of Donnacona and his sons, and the next month

**MAY** Cartier leaves on his third voyage with a large group of colonists
**AUGUST** Cartier establishes a settlement, Charlesbourg-Royal, near Stadacona, and again is unable to navigate the river beyond the rapids at Hochelaga

**SEPTEMBER** Cartier dies at his estate outside Saint-Malo

**1542**

**1541**

**1557**

**JUNE** Cartier disobeys Roberval's orders to return to Charlesbourg-Royal and sails to France, arriving in September reaches the village of Hochelaga, where he is forced to turn back.

**1535–1536**  Cartier and his party winter near Stadacona.

**1536**  MAY  Cartier and crew, with Donnacona and his sons, set sail for France, returning in July.

**1541**  MAY  Cartier leaves on his third voyage with a large group of colonists, although his superior, Roberval, is not yet ready to leave.

AUGUST  Cartier establishes a settlement, Charles-bourg-Royal, near Stadacona, and again is unable to navigate the river beyond the rapids at Hochelaga.

**1541–1542**  The colonists survive another harsh winter.

**1542**  JUNE  Cartier abandons camp and encounters Roberval. He disobeys Roberval's orders to return to Charlesbourg-Royal and sails to France, arriving in September.

**1557**  SEPTEMBER  Cartier dies at his estate outside Saint-Malo.

# GLOSSARY

ARCHAEOLOGISTS  scientists who study ancient civilizations

ASTRONOMY  the study of the stars; astronomy was important to early sailors so they could navigate at sea by looking at the stars

CHAPLAINS  members of the clergy, often assigned to military units

FLEUR-DE-LIS  a representation of a lily that was the official symbol of the royalty of France, and is still an unofficial symbol of that nation

INTERPRETER  someone who speaks two or more languages and can be used as a go-between for people who speak different languages

LATITUDE  an imaginary line that marks horizontal points around the globe; latitude and longitude (vertical lines) are important measurements for seagoing vessels

LEAGUE  an old form of measuring distance, marking the length a typical man could walk in one hour; a league is equal to about 3.5 miles, or 5.5 km

LIVRES  a measure of currency in France during Cartier's time

MARINER  someone who works at sea for a living

MIDDLE AGES  the period of European history roughly from the fifth century to the fifteenth century; also called the Medieval Period or the Dark Ages, it came before the Renaissance

NAUTICAL MILES  a measure of distance used at sea; 1 nautical mile is equal to 1.15 miles or 1.85 km on land

NORSEMAN   people from northern Europe, especially Scandinavia, who lived roughly from the late eighth century to the eleventh century; some Norsemen were also called Vikings

NORTHWEST PASSAGE   the passage that early explorers imagined existed through North America to Asia

RED OCHER   a paint or pigment made from crushed minerals

RENAISSANCE   the period of European history extending roughly from the fifteenth century to the seventeenth century; characterized by great advances in the arts, culture, sciences, and exploration

SCURVY   a serious and sometimes fatal disease caused by a lack of vitamin C

WITHERED   shrunken or shriveled

# BIBLIOGRAPHY

Cumming, W.P., S. Hiller, D.B. Quinn, and G. Williams. *The Exploration of North America 1630–1776*. New York: G.P. Putnam's Sons, 1974.

Dawson, Samuel Edward. *The Saint Lawrence: Its Basin and Border-Lands*. New York: Stokes, 1905.

Dougherty, Kevin. "Long-lost Jacques Cartier settlement rediscovered at Quebec City." *CanWest News Service*, August 19, 2006. Reprinted on Canada.com. Available online at http://www.canada.com/topics/news/national/story.html?id=4978e603-f67e-4784-807d-7f3911c60829&k=27303&p=2.

Eccles, W.J. *The Canadian Frontier 1534–1760*. New York: Holt, Reinhart, 1969.

———. *The French in North America 1500–1783*. East Lansing: Michigan State University Press, 1998.

Jaenen, Cornelius J. *Friend and Foe: Aspects of French-Amerindian Cultural Contact in the Sixteenth and Seventeenth Centuries*. New York: Columbia University Press, 1976.

Leacock, Stephen. *The Mariner of Saint-Malo*. Toronto: Glasgow, Brook, 1914.

Moogk, Peter N. *La Nouvelle France: the Making of French Canada—A Cultural History*. East Lansing: Michigan State University Press, 2000.

Oleson, Tryggvi J. *Early Voyages and Northern Approaches, 1000–1632*. Toronto: McClellan and Stewart, 1963.

Parkman, Francis. *The Parkman Reader*. Boston: Little, Brown, 1955.

Richter, Daniel K. *Facing East from Indian Country: A Native History of Early America*. Cambridge, Mass.: Harvard University Press, 2000.

Trudel, Marcel. *The Beginnings of New France 1524–1663*. Toronto: McClelland and Stewart, 1973.

# FURTHER RESOURCES

Blashfield, Jean F. *Cartier: Jacques Cartier in Search of the Northwest Passage*. Minneapolis, Minn.: Compass Point, 2002.

Cooke, Tim. *The St. Lawrence River*. Milwaukee: Gareth Stevens Publishing, 2003.

Crompton, Samuel Willard. *Robert de la Salle*. New York: Chelsea House, 2009.

Dickinson, John A. *A Short History of Quebec*. Quebec: McGill-Queen's University Press (4e), 2008.

Hamilton, Janice. *The St. Lawrence River: History, Highway, and Habitat*. Montreal: Redlader Publishing, 2006.

Koestler-Grack, Rachel A. *Ferdinand Magellan*. New York: Chelsea House, 2009.

Lace, William W. *Captain James Cook*. New York: Chelsea House, 2009.

———. *Sir Francis Drake*. New York: Chelsea House, 2009.

Lackey, Jennifer. *Exploring the St. Lawrence River*. New York: Crabtree Publishing, 2006.

Worth, Richard. *Vasco da Gama*. New York: Chelsea House, 2009.

## FILMS

*The Empire of the Bay* (DVD) PBS Homevideo

*Mes Voyages en Canada de Jacques Cartier* ("My Discoveries in Canada by Jacques Cartier") (DVD) Canadian documentary

## WEB SITES

### The Early French Exploration and Settlement: Inventing New France

http://brown.edu/Facilities/John_Carter_Brown_Library/Champlain exhib/Pages/Inventing+.html

*This site, maintained by Brown University, reproduces many fascinating old drawings and maps connected to Cartier's journeys.*

### "Empire of the Bay: Who Were the Pathfinders?": PBS

http://www.pbs.org/empireofthebay/profiles/cartier.html

*A look into the lives of the explorers and others who were central to the Hudson's Bay Company. Features maps, biographies of explorers (including Jacques Cartier), quizzes, and forums.*

### European Explorers: Jacques Cartier

http://www.cdli.ca/CITE/excartier.htm

*Maintained by a Canadian schoolteacher, this portal offers a wealth of information on Jacques Cartier.*

### Explorers, Pioneers, and Frontiersmen, 1491–1557: Jacques Cartier

http://www.u-s-history.com/about.html

*This "online highway" enriches travelers' experiences by providing history and other types of background information. The site is supported by Travel and History and includes quizzes, glossary, maps, and tables.*

### Jacques Cartier

http://www.elizabethan-era.org.uk/jacques-cartier.htm

*Interesting facts and historical bits about Jacques Cartier. Also links to information about the Age of Exploration and the Elizabethan Era.*

### Québec

http://www.gouv.qc.ca/portail/quebec/pgs/commun/?lang=en

*A site sponsored by the government of Quebec. Provides general information about the services offered to citizens, businesses, and international clients of the government of Quebec.*

### St. Lawrence River: A History

http://www.vsr.cape.com/~powens/riverhistory.htm

*The history of one of the world's great rivers. The site includes black and white and color photographs, links to other sites that focus on Canadian history, and a bibliography.*

# PICTURE CREDITS

# INDEX

# ABOUT THE AUTHOR

**ADAM WOOG** has written more than 60 books for adults, young adults, and children. He has special interests in history and biography. Woog did his undergraduate work at Simon Fraser University in Burnaby, British Columbia, where he first became interested in Canadian history. He also holds a master's degree in communication from Antioch University. Woog lives in his hometown of Seattle, Washington, with his wife and their daughter.